Methadone Clinic

By

David Steier

authorHOUSE™

1663 LIBERTY DRIVE, SUITE 200
BLOOMINGTON, INDIANA 47403
(800) 839-8640
WWW.AUTHORHOUSE.COM

© 2005 David Steier
All Rights Reserved.

No part of this book may be reproduced, stored in a retrieval system, or transmitted by any means without the written permission of the author.

First published by AuthorHouse 05/30/05

ISBN: 1-4184-9872-6 (sc)

Library of Congress Control Number: 2004097803

Printed in the United States of America
Bloomington, Indiana

This book is printed on acid-free paper.

AUTHOR'S NOTE

Methadone Clinic is not meant to be a commentary on the value or efficacy of methadone maintenance treatment.

It is instead, a novelized true-to-life account of my experiences as a substance abuse counselor at a major New York City methadone clinic.

From December 1992 until May 1995, I was an integral part of this obscure world.

I was driven to write this book because I know that I have an interesting and important story to tell.

Methadone Clinic will give you a behind the scenes look into the plight of the patients and the workers who dwell within this domain, and as such, I believe that it is also a book of significant social import.

In essence, it is a gritty slice of life, and it is my hope that the reader will be enlightened, entertained, and perhaps even moved by this work.

Finally, it is important to stress that absolutely no confidentialities have been violated. I have taken great care to be fair and ethical, and I fully understand and respect the sanctity of the patient/counselor relationship.

Thank you for reading *Methadone Clinic*.

1

I didn't know what to do. I had no job, no money, and no prospects. All I had left was some food, my clothes, several pairs of shoes, a television, a stereo, and my books. That was it, and the way things were going, pretty soon I'd have to hock the TV and the stereo. It wasn't good.

A few days earlier I had cashed my last unemployment check and now I was scared. Me, Billy Selkirk.

Man, I thought, it sure is easy to fall by the wayside. Once ya hit da skids ya just keep skiddin' 'til ya hit skid row.

Unfortunately, there wasn't even a skid row anymore—those damn yuppie assholes took care of that back in the '80s when they gentrified the Bowery.

It was a bright and sunny summer day in late August, but I just sat in my dirty underwear, lethargic and miserable, smoking cigarette after cigarette. Even when I ran out of smokes I couldn't get off my big fat pasty-white Irish ass. Ordinarily, as soon as I ran out I'd go and get some more, but this time I just kept looking out of my living room window, which didn't help my mood any.

During the hour or so that I sat there I observed a shopping bag lady take a shit behind a dumpster, I saw these three winos fight over a bottle, and I watched the cops hassle this poor old guy selling Puerto Rican ices from this crazy looking pushcart.

Nature rules, so when I had to take a vicious piss, I finally got up. As I drained my bladder I decided to splurge on a pack of Marlboros instead of generics, and for some reason this made me feel a little better.

I threw on a thin T-shirt, slipped into an old pair of worn out blue denim shorts, grabbed my wallet and split. The second I hit the streets I regretted leaving the building. The heat and humidity had merged with the pre-existing urban potpourri of smog, sweat, dog shit and everything else that was vile and disgusting, making me sick to my stomach. I was going to run right back into my building, but then I remembered that I was running low on beer and that I had to get the *Times*, so I trodded on.

As I walked towards the neighborhood bodega, I passed a group of homeless bums who were camped out in Tompkins Square Park. New York's a wart hog from hell in the summer, in large part due to them, and like most New Yorkers I wished that they would all just disappear.

In the hot weather those motherfuckers turned the city into a urine sauna, and compassion has its limits. These creatures were like aliens from parts unknown, clad in their many layers of grimy shirts, sweaters and coats during the hottest months of the year. Wine sores, skin ulcers, and public urination made them even more popular and we were all very lucky, because even when they dropped like flies, there was an endless supply of them. This was New York and they were a given. Sigh.

I made it to the store, got everything and headed back. I laughed out loud when this one homeless guy lost control of his shopping cart and it hit a parked cab.

Okay, I'll admit it, at least they're good for a laugh. Those carts were funny, the funniest thing about those bums. As far as anyone knew, they stole the carts from supermarkets, which was funny in and of itself. They would always be filled to the brim with useless crap; stuff like broken radios, empty boxes, old magazines, and cruddy clothes.

I hoped that the poor bastard got away before the cabbie got a hold of him, and for a fleeting moment I even felt a little sorry for the skell, but with all of my worries that notion passed fast.

My apartment was almost as hot as the streets and the old box fan didn't do much, but I tried to make the best of it and flipped open a beer. I smoked three more cigarettes and took out the *Times* want ads. I looked over the job listings and quickly discovered that since I was a computer illiterate I was unemployable. In frustration, I threw the whole fucking paper on the floor and cursed myself for being such a hopeless moron.

After I got tired of sulking I remembered that I hadn't eaten breakfast, so I had some black coffee and chocolate pop tarts. It was only 11:30. I checked my wallet and I had about two hundred bucks, which wouldn't have been so bad if it wasn't my entire net worth. Thirty years old and this is all I have. What a loser.

I thought about my options for the day, and then I decided to go to Coney Island Beach. The beach was free, and lunch at Nathan's was cheap.

I took a shower, changed into my beach clothes, and left the tenement at noon. I was wearing a tie-dyed tank top, a pair of baggy trunks, sandals, sunglasses, and this funky old Panama hat. I carried this great big blue, green, and white beach towel that featured a distinctly tropical Puerto Rican motif, which made sense since I bought it in a neighborhood schlock shop.

As I walked down St. Mark's Place to the F train in the West Village, this girl named Pamm spotted me. Pamm, spelled P-A-M-M. Why she spelled it this way I didn't know and didn't care, because all I wanted to do was avoid her. This, however, was impossible. She was sitting on a stoop near the corner of 4th Avenue, within twenty feet of me, so I hesitated for a moment and then sat down next to her. I had no choice.

She was 17, or so she said, but she looked even younger. In fact, if you didn't know better you never would have guessed that she was a runaway and a junky whore, and I wondered how long it would take before she started looking like one.

I knew Pamm from the neighborhood the same way that I knew the dry cleaner, the shoemaker, and bodega owner. I knew her the same way that I knew old Ukrainian lady who swept up in front of the building every day and the same way that I knew a hundred other people—hello, goodbye.

Okay, so maybe not exactly the same way, and how such a sweet young thing could wind up blowing guys like me in some back alley at four in the morning was a tragedy, but I was on the go and I wasn't in the mood for her.

I was as nice as I could be, but after a few minutes of cigarettes and bullshit I got up to go. So you're blonde and young and hot—I don't care, I gotta go.

"Okay Pamm, I'll see ya later. I'm goin' to Coney Island and it's a long ride. I wanna get there while it's still hot. 'Bye."

"YOU'RE GOING TO THE BEACH? OOH— LEMME COME WITH YOU!" she shouted, grabbing my arm.

Oh man, how am I gonna get outta this? So she's hot looking. I don't care. I'm not into this. What am I gonna do?

"Uh, Pamm, today's not a good day. Maybe one day next week. Okay?"

"NEXT WEEK? FUCK YOU, NEXT WEEK. HOW ABOUT NEXT YEAR? HOW ABOUT NEVER? FUCK YOU, BILLY!"

Oh boy. I guess she really wants to go to the beach. I must have stood there for a full minute, just staring at her, not knowing what to say. Her face was red and sweaty and her hair was flying all over the place, but she still looked beautiful. She really did.

Pamm stood at about 5' 4", and her silky blonde hair fell down to her shoulders. It varied in tones from platinum to dark honey and was striking, and together with her small perky nose, her luminous blue-green eyes, and her great shape, she was irresistible.

"I'm sorry, Pamm. I didn't realize how much you wanted to go. You can come."

"Ah, forget it."

"Oh, c'mon. Don't be like that. I want you to come with me. There's just one thing."

"What?"

"Your clothes. Railroad boots, black jeans and a black T-shirt. Not exactly beach attire."

"Shut up Billy. Let's go."

We walked along, side by side, and when we got to the corner of 8th Street and 6th Avenue, in the heart of the West Village, she stops in front of this super drugstore and tells me to wait.

She says that she'll be out in a few minutes and runs inside. A short time later she darts out of the store, runs up to me and grabs my hand. She starts pulling me but I don't move.

"LET'S GO! C'MON!"

"Wait a second. You're acting weird. What's with you?"

"C'mon—we gotta go. I just ripped off that Duane Reade store for a swimsuit. I took off the security tag and I put it on. I'm wearing it under my clothes—Oh, do me a favor—take this."

She pulls out a pair of white cotton panties from her back pocket and hands them to me. I dutifully take 'em and stuff 'em in my beach towel.

"Don't look at me that way Billy—just because I pinched a cheap swimsuit it doesn't mean that I'm a lowlife."

"I didn't say anything, Pamm. Don't be so sensitive."

"Yeah, well, don't look at me like that. I just wanna have a good time today. Is that okay with you?"

"Shut up Pamm—you're getting on my nerves. Let's go before I change my mind."

We continued to walk to the train, ignoring each other but still together. Oh well, I thought, we'll probably have a rotten day but at least she'll look good on the beach.

2

The Stillwell Avenue subway station is a total gross-out. Big, dank, and dirty, it's a major link in the chain of the city's rapid transit system, and it's a world unto itself.

Within its confines lie several snack bars and newsstands, a police station, and a diner that's located at the station's main entrance, right off Surf Avenue.

I love this joint. The place has atmosphere and gritty style and red padded stools that swivel all the way around. No tables or booths, just a long, wide counter dotted by pastry cases and ashtrays. High above the grill there's a no smoking sign taped to the aluminum wall, but try telling that to the crackheads and street prostitutes who frequent the place.

I wanted to eat here but Pamm said no. No? No. Why not? EWW! IT'S DISGUSTING! It's not disgusting, Pamm—just a little skeevy. Like how many places still serve oxtail stew? What are you talking about Billy? Forget it Pamm—let's go to Nathan's.

We walked across the street to Nathan's and I bought us franks, fries, and cokes from this sweaty counterman who looked like Curly from the Three Stooges, and we had our lunch. We ate standing up at one of the stainless steel counters, al fresco, just like everyone else. It was cool to take in the scene with its carnival feel and eat lunch at the same time.

After we finished eating we strolled down 17th Street towards the beach, and along the way I stopped off at this Pakistani convenience store for some beer. On a whim I bought two 40 ounce bottles of malt liquor instead, and when I gave one to Pamm she got pissed.

"What is this shit?" she blurted out.

"It's Olde English 800—Puerto Rican rocket fuel. It's strong—stronger than beer."

"Never heard of it."

"So? Who gives a shit if you've never heard of it? Just shuddup and drink it."

She opened her bottle in its brown paper bag and took a swig. Then, she made a face and went off on me.

"I hate this shit—it's nasty. I like Rolling Rock. Why'd you buy this shit anyway? You said that you were gonna get us beer. What the fuck is wrong with you?"

"Take it or leave it."

I walked away from her and sat down on the curb. I opened my bottle and took a few swallows. Moments later she joined me. At least she knew when to back down.

"Next time I'll buy you champagne, Princess."

"Shut up, Fats."

With that, she poked me in the gut and we both laughed. Then, we continued down 17th until we hit the beach. We stopped near the water, spread out the towel and settled in.

Pamm took off her street clothes and she looked GOOD. That aqua metallic bikini that she pinched did her justice. Her firm, supple titties oozed confidence, and her ass was to die for.

She didn't have enough fat on her to fry an egg. Surprisingly, there were no tattoos, which was rare for an East Village chick. I had never seen her this way before, and to put it mildly, I was impressed.

At least one of us looked good. The brutal orange-yellow sunlight told no lies, and with my big fat chalky-white belly hanging over my baggy trunks, I looked like a Southern sheriff. Even worse, I had almost no muscle tone, but I did have these tufts of coarse black hair growing wild and free around my tits. Hmm, maybe one day I'd get into shape. Yeah, right.

To my relief, things were working out well. We talked, we swam, we walked along the ocean, and we dozed in the sun. Then, about an hour before we left, Pamm came up with this skinny little joint and we finished it in less than ten minutes. The weed was pretty good, and as we gazed at the sea and watched the seagulls forage for scraps, Pamm mentioned that she was enrolled in some kind of drug program.

I knew that she did heroin but I never gave it much thought. All the kids in the East Village were doing it. Her "program" was this methadone clinic somewhere in Queens. She said that she hadn't done dope in a long time, and from the looks of her arms that appeared to be true. You had to look very closely to see even the faintest old needle mark.

3

Before we left for the city we spent some time on the boardwalk. Everyone loves the boardwalk, a two and one half mile expanse that starts at West 37th Street and ends up at the foot of Manhattan Beach.

In recent years Natalie Merchant, LFO, and the Lemonheads have all shot videos on the Coney Island boardwalk, and long ago even Trotsky paid a visit. True, Coney ain't what it used to be, but it still remains a world famous locale with a lot to offer.

It was in this spirit that I took Pamm to the Atlantis for a beer. The Atlantis is a cool bar because there's no other dive in the city quite like it. The whole dump opens out on to the boardwalk; no doors, just a great big wide entrance.

There were plenty of available booths but we sat at the long oak bar instead, where we enjoyed a clear, unobstructed view of the water. The old Puerto Rican bartender didn't bother to ID Pamm, which really wasn't too surprising. People from places like Coney Island don't like asking a lot of questions.

So here we were, drinking our tap beers and smoking our cigarettes, just a couple of normal freaks hanging out. I hadn't had a day as good as this one in quite a while, but soon it was time to go. When the sun began to set we left, walking north towards the Aquarium, where we crossed the overpass and caught the train at the West 8th Street station.

When we got back to the city, things got awkward. As we walked toward the nabe I got the feeling that Pamm was up to something, and I'm sure that she sensed my apprehension.

Not sure what to do, I invited her for coffee at the Odessa, my favorite East Village restaurant, thinking that this would be a good place to end the day.

I loved this cafe because it was a neighborhood institution. They served up a whole lotta food for very little money and they left you alone. They never bugged you, even after five or six coffee refills, and it didn't even matter if there were people waiting to be seated. Everybody gets their turn and if you can't wait you can go somewhere else. Tough.

I ordered coffee and babka for me and an egg cream and plain donut for Pamm. Oh yeah, she was up to something all right—But what? A flip of her hair, a seemingly unconscious handling of her tits—Oh, Jesus.

There was this palpable tension in the air as we smoked our cigarettes and made forced conversation. Then, all of a sudden she runs out of gas—she has nothing left to say and neither do I, so for a few seconds we just sit there and stare at each other. I signaled the waitress and she came over and gave me the check.

"Pamm, we had a pretty good time today. Right?"

"Yeah, Billy, I did have a good time. Thanks for the beers and the food and all. I just hope that I wasn't a pest."

"Stop it—I had a great time. In fact, let's do it again before the summer's over. Okay?"

"Sure. Thanks Billy."

"Good. So I guess we'll call it a day."

"That's a wonderful idea—you'll go back to your place and I'll go back to my squat."

"I figured that you lived in a squat. A lotta people around here do."

"Yeah, and a lotta people around here also eat outta garbage cans. At least I don't have to do that."

"Oh c'mon Pamm. Don't lay this guilt trip on me. I'm just one step away from the street myself."

"Don't worry Billy, I'm not homeless. I'm doin' just fine. I live in a squat with some other girls and a couple of guys. Actually, I don't really know how many people I live with. People just sort of come and go. But it's great because it's free and one of the dudes even knows how to steal electricity, so we have a fan, a TV and a CD player. Maybe one day we'll even have a computer. Who knows?"

"Awesome. I'm glad everything's copasetic."

"What's that supposed to mean?"

"Copasetic; ya know, cool."

Uh oh. I shouldn't have said that. Suddenly, Pamm's face turns bright tomato red as she freaks out, screaming at me, with tears streaming down her cheeks and snot dripping out of her nose. She was making a scene.

Before it got any worse, instinct kicked in. I threw a five on the table, grabbed her by the arm and we split.

We crossed the street and sat on the steps of St. Bridget's Roman Catholic Church. While I waited for her to stop crying I lit a cigarette, took a drag, and gave it to her. She took it and smoked it and finally started to calm down. After several more cigarettes she grabbed my big beach towel and wiped her face with it. Boy, was she a sight.

Under the neon glare with her face all red and her hair all disheveled, she was scary. So much so, that I almost shit in my pants when she went off on me again.

"BILLY YOU FUCKHEAD—YOU DON'T GIVE A DAMN ABOUT ME AND NOBODY ELSE DOES EITHER!" she sobbed.

She sobbed all right, loud wracking sobs. For a moment it even sounded like she had the dry heaves.

"Billy, I'm sorry if you think I'm crazy, but you're my last hope. I gotta get outta that fuckin' hellhole. You don't know what it's like. I can't take it anymore. Please lemme stay with you—even if it's only for a couple of weeks. Please?"

"Hold on Pamm—lemme think for a minute. Okay?"

"Okay."

I smoked a Marb and I tried to think but I couldn't. Pamm was waiting for an answer and I was on the spot. Big time. I had to say something, but what?

"Um, Pamm, ya know I'm just a regular guy and I'd like to help you, but how do I know that I can trust you?"

"Lemme tell you something Billy. Last night I was scared shitless when I was woke up by a rat. This big fat slimy rat was crawling right near my head. IT WAS ALMOST ON MY FACE! I THOUGHT I WAS GONNA DIE!!"

"Christ almighty. What happened next?"

"I started screaming and I woke everybody up. They all cursed me out, and this one ugly fat bitch said that she was gonna kick my ass and she lunged at me but the guys grabbed her—this one dude actually slapped her. Hard, too. Right in her fucking ugly face. Next, she's sitting there crying, I'm still in shock over this fuckin' rodent, and everyone else is just kind of standing around. It's about four in the morning and I'm in this disgusting squat with these five or six other other lunatics, I don't even know how many, and now all I know is, is that I gotta get outta there, so I took my money and split."

"Where did you go?"

"I went to the Kiev for coffee and donuts and hung out there for an hour or so. Then, I just sort of hung out in the street until I bumped into you. I'm lucky I didn't get raped. Billy, I'm not making this stuff up and I'm not stupid enough or nasty enough to fuck you over for helping me. Now can I stay with you?"

"Hmm. From what you're tellin' me you didn't get any sleep last night. If I said no you'd fall asleep in the gutter and that would be that. C'mon, let's get moving."

"Oh, Billy, thank you. I thought you were gonna say no."

"Yeah, well, just don't fuck up."

"Shut up Billy."

4

Pamm held on to my hand and wouldn't let go until we entered my building. I felt a little funny as I unlocked the door to my apartment, but it was a done deal, and there was no way to weasel out of it now.

I put the beach towel with the panties inside on the kitchen table, and took her for a walk around the place. She wasn't very impressed, but the prospect of taking a shower pleased her, so while she showered I had a beer.

I spent a pensive ten minutes or so drinking beer out of my favorite mug, and thought about my heady day. Pamm. Man. What the hell have I gotten myself into? She's a runaway, a drug addict, and a street ho. The skinny bitch tells me a sob story and I cave so she's here. Nice going.

Oh, great, and now she's yelling at m̶ ̶ ̶m̶ the toilet. *What?* Get me my panties and some c̶ *My clothes?* Just for tonight. I'll get my s̶ squat tomorrow. *All right.* Thanks, Billy.

I grabbed the beach towel with the panties inside and went to the bedroom and found some denim shorts and a black T-shirt. I knocked on the bathroom door and she opened it a crack and I clumsily shoved it all at her.

"HEY!"

"Sorry. Listen—those shorts should be okay. Size 30 waist from when I was skinny. Anyway, it's all clean."

Five minutes later we were sharing a joint at the kitchen table and discussing our plans for the next day. Pamm was anxious about getting her things out of the squat and it didn't take a genius to understand why. I even offered to go with her.

"You mean you would do that for me?"

"Yeah, why not? What's the big deal? I don't think any of those mutants will fuck with you if I come along. I know I'm not tough, but I'm still a pretty big guy."

"True. And if you come with me I won't have to worry about gettin' mugged on the walk home, either. I mean a good lookin' white girl carrying bags of clothes n' stuff in the worst part of the East Village. Boy, Billy, thanks."

"No problem. Look, I gotta get some sleep. I'm going to bed."

"Yeah, I wanna go to bed, too. Where am I gonna sleep?"

"You can sleep on the futon in the living room. It pulls out. Take whatever you need for bed outta the linen closet. Turn up the fan if you want. Okay?"

"It's more than okay. For the first time in months I'll be able to sleep with both eyes closed."

"Yeah, and you can sleep as late as you want. Now lemme go to bed."

"Good night, Billy."

"Good night, Pamm."

5

We were both up early the next morning, and after some coffee and stale biscotti that Pamm had dug up from a corner in the icebox, we made a run for it. Pamm couldn't wait to get her things, and a short time later we were at the squat.

The building was on a block with other like structures of once noble bearing, all seemingly abandoned and unoccupied. Here and there some homeless bum or shopping bag lady loitered about on the desolate stretch, which offered yet another vision of New York City hell.

As we gingerly made our way up the stairs of the boarded up beige brick hovel that Pamm had once called home, I wanted to vomit. YECCH! The stench was indescribable, it was hot as hell, and by the time we hit the fourth floor apartment I was catatonic. So much so, that I hardly moved when Pamm pushed open the door and a cluster of rats scurried away.

The squat was a big four room flat, and I'm guessing that in its heyday the building wasn't half-bad, but that was then and this was now. All I wanted was for her to get her stuff and for us to get the fuck out.

"C'MON, PAMM—GET YOUR THINGS! C'MON! THIS PLACE REEKS!"

"Stop it Billy. Just gimme two minutes."

"I can't wait two minutes. I'm not kidding—I can't. There's no one up here to hassle you—I'll wait for you outside."

Before she had a chance to answer I ran down the stairs as fast as I could and waited on the stoop. While pigeons pecked at specks of debris, I nervously paced back and forth. A few minutes later Pamm emerged with a scowl and a couple of plastic bags.

"Boy, are you a pussy. I can't believe you cut out like that."

"I couldn't help it. If I stayed up there any longer I would have thrown up."

"Baby."

"Bitch. Anyways, did you get everything?"

"Yeah. I even found my works."

"Your works? I thought you stopped doin' dope."

"I have. At least for now. I'm on a methadone program and I'm trying to be a good girl. I need my works in case I can't hack it. Try to understand."

"I will. Look, let's get moving. How about some coffee and donuts at that place on B and Fourth?"

"Cool. It'll be like a little celebration. Right?"

"Right. Let's go."

Pamm gave me the bags and as we walked along she took my left hand just like she had done the night before. I didn't know what to make of this and it puzzled me. Does she think I'm her boyfriend? Her sugar daddy? Her rescuer? I dunno man, I dunno.

We sat at the counter of the coffee shoppe and I ordered two light coffees and four assorted donuts. I placed her two bags on the floor, wedging them between my feet and shins.

We ate our donuts and sipped our coffee and sat there silently. Bored, I glanced at the welfare mom with the two kids cramming donuts in their faces; I saw a shopping bag lady pick butts out of ashtrays; and, worst of all, I caught a glimpse of myself in the mirror behind the counter.

Man, did I look beat. My full head of dark brown hair was all over the place; a full head of cowlicks. My face was none the better for two days beard growth, and my blue eyes were red. I looked like a bum.

At least my looks didn't seem to bother Pamm, as she wiped her sweaty forehead with a clump of napkins and then dropped the clump on the floor. How refined. True, this place made rats retch, but c'mon. I had to say something.

"Pamm, why did you throw that on the floor? What the fuck is with you?"

"Oh, shuddup Billy. I have more important things to talk to you about."

"Like what?"

"Like I know where you can get a job."

"Big deal. I also know where I can get a job. This greasy spoon always needs help. So does the supermarket across the street. So?"

"So you're such an asshole. I'm not talking about a peon job. What I'm saying is, is that you could be a substance abuse counselor at my clinic."

"Oh please."

"Don't 'Oh please' me. It's not such a bad job."

"What makes you think I'm qualified? I don't have any experience."

She picked some crumbs off of the paper plate and put them in my empty coffee cup. Then, she gives me the sly eye and shakes her head in mock disbelief.

"You don't know what the fuck you're talking about. Take my word for it. They always need counselors."

"If that's the case, then the job must suck."

"Most jobs suck."

"Yeah, I'll grant ya that. Whadda ya havta do, anyway?"

"You have to work with people like me. You have to help the patients get what they need from the program. You could do it."

"Na-ah, I don't think that I'd like a place like that. It sounds creepy."

"Look you idiot, they like their counselors to have college degrees and you have a college degree. Any major is fine. You have a B.A. I'm sure they'd take you."

"From the way you tell it, it sounds like they'd take anyone."

"I don't mean it to sound that way, Billy. And no, they won't just take anyone. Not anymore, anyway. Too many counselors have quit on them after a few days, or weeks, or months and they've had it with that shit. They need people who'll work out and I think that you'd work out."

Hmm, maybe she was right, but even if she wasn't, her heart was in the right place, and it was a white collar job.

After a long, thoughtful pause, I playfully tweaked her left titty, and before she had a chance to knock my hand away, I told her that we'd talk about it at home. I tossed some money on the counter and we left the coffee shoppe.

Once we got back we just kind of lounged around. It was disgusting outside, all hot and sticky and humid, but since I had a third floor apartment the place wasn't too bad. I had the big box fan going and a nice breeze came in through the living room window.

Both of us were exhausted, so we put all the heavy talk on hold and tried to enjoy the rest of the day. We were more than happy to get stoned on Pamm's pot, listen to music, pig out on whatever I had, and get stoned again. It was good to forget about our troubles for a while.

By late evening Pamm was fast asleep on the futon and I was nodding off in my recliner, so I called it a day and went to bed. It was our second night together.

6

The next morning after breakfast Pamm wrote down the address and phone number of her methadone clinic on the front page of my *Daily News*, and urged me to call for an interview. Since my options were few, and my expectations of ever getting anything good out of life almost totally dashed anyway, I decided to do it.

As soon as Pamm went out for cigarettes I dialed the number of the "Jackson Heights Treatment and Rehabilitation Clinic", located in Jackson Heights, Queens. Someone picked up the phone on the third ring. I asked for the personnel office and was put on hold by some gruff voiced black guy. Then, after a short wait, this woman named Colleen got on.

I was all nervous and mealy mouthed, but I did manage to ask her if there were any counseling positions available. She said yes, and then she asked me if I was a college graduate. I told her that I had a bachelor's degree in sociology, which was true, and said that I was very interested in the field of substance abuse counseling, which wasn't.

Next, she puts me on hold for a minute or so, and when she gets back on she gets right to the point. She says that I should come in that day for an interview, and when I hesitate for a moment she gets very irritated. She tells me to call back when I'm ready to make an appointment, but a second before she's about to hang up I ask her what time she'd like me to come in. She hurriedly gives me the address that Pamm had already given to me and tells me to be there at two. I thank her, she hangs up, and now I'm nervous.

It's about 12:15. I have less than two hours to get cleaned up, dressed up, and make it over there. I take a three minute shower, shave, and put on my clothes. I wear my only suit, the dark blue wool funeral job— perfect for a hot summer day. Under the jacket I'm wearing my brightest white shirt and a wide but thin red and black tie. I slip on a pair of stiff black loafers with tassels over black nylon socks, place some old resumes in a large clasp envelope and I'm out the door by 1 p.m. sharp. Not bad.

An instant later I hit the cracked sidewalk and I don't look back. All I want to do is to catch the train to Jackson Heights and get there on time. It's torturously hot, I hate the clothes that I'm wearing and I sure as hell ain't ready for this.

Nevertheless, a few minutes later I'm standing on the platform waiting for the F train to Queens.

While I wait for the train I spot this fat black transit worker in an orange mesh vest throwing peanuts to the rats scurrying on the tracks, and I'm reminded of Pamm's rat story. YIKES!! Those raggedy little motherfuckers are terrifying. Poor Pamm.

At the same time that this jerk is feeding the animals, some shoeless bum is taking a whizz down by the far end. None of this shit is too unusual for the hellhole subways but it's still gross and I'm in no fucking mood for it and I wish that the scumbag would piss directly on the third rail and electrocute himself, the motherfucker.

Just before the rats were finished eating and the skell had a chance to shake off the last few drops, the train pulls in. I manage to find a seat and I squirm around wishing that this goddamn day was over. I bury my head in my hands and try to relax.

I wonder what I'm getting myself into because it's weird to get an immediate job interview, especially in New York, and especially for a job where they ask you if you have a college degree. I'm filled with anxiety and apprehension, and as I head towards my destination I think to myself, "Just what kind of fuckin' place is this?"

7

I get off the train when the train hits the Jackson Heights stop and I take out the slip of paper with the address on it. I climb up the subway stairs and stagger out on to the street, and suddenly I'm in the middle of this noisy Colombian neighborhood and I'm lost. I search fruitlessly for the clinic, and as I'm about to give up I spot this off-white, nondescript building about three blocks away from Roosevelt Avenue, the main drag.

Could this be the place? It's the right address but something seems off—it's as if they want to keep the place a secret. Is it a cathouse? There are so many of 'em around here that I wouldn't be surprised. Maybe this is Pamm's idea of a joke—fuck it; it's the same address that the lady from the clinic gave me when I called, so I'm going in.

I happen to notice the closed circuit TV camera mounted over the building's solid steel door, and as the sweat soaks through my best shirt I press the button and after a very long minute I'm buzzed in.

I timidly walk up to this weird, freaky looking reception desk that sits high off the floor. The fuckin' desk isn't even a desk, it's actually a black and hot orange dry bar that belongs in some South Bronx basement, not a medical facility.

I tell the prick at the desk why I'm there and he rudely orders me to sit down and wait. I don't like this guy or this place, I think, as I take a seat on this uncomfortable hardwood navy blue bench.

Several minutes pass and as my misgivings grow and I'm lost in thought, the guy at the desk gives me permission to go to the business office. I do as he says and walk down this narrow corridor and stop when I reach this wooden half-door with a wide countertop.

An attractive blonde with big tits greets me. She asks me if I'm Billy Selkirk and I nod yes. I wonder if this is Colleen and indeed it is. She opens the half-door, seats me at her desk and gives me an application to fill out. After I complete it she tells me that I'll be interviewed by Selma Hack, the assistant administrator, but that it might be a while.

During the wait some dried up old bag of about 60 or so, walks up to the half-door and starts ranting and raving about "my bottles." Colleen warns her that she better shut up or she'll get thrown off the program, and the old lady slinks away, muttering curse words under her breath. Jesus, this place is already making me shudder.

Genius that I am, I figure out that the half-door serves as a sort of low level protective device for the benefit of the office staff. I also learn from Colleen that the guys who man the reception desk are know "deskmen", and that a deskman functions as a security guard-slash-assistant to the dispensing nurses.

As I wait and wait for Selma I pass the time hating myself, wishing that I could have done better in life. Why can't I just be a normal guy and get a normal job and make some real money? Why can't I be a stockbroker or a lawyer or an engineer? Why did I have to have these two cold, anal retentive Irish Catholic idiots for parents who would have been doing me a favor if they had put me up for adoption. WHY? WHY? WHY?

I don't believe in God, but if there is a God then he's a real prick, I think bitterly, at which point Selma Hack waltzes in, proving my point.

Colleen introduces me to Selma and my intuition tells me that this lady is a real piece of work. Selma was in her early fifties and by appearances I judged her to be of German descent.

Without smiling she stuck out her clammy right hand and I shook it, trying not to stare at the pockmarks on her cheeks and the several fine dark hairs that sprouted from her chin. She stood at about 5' 6" but she seemed taller, and her aquiline nose, steel-blue eyes and reddish brown hair completed the package. I wondered if she was a former heroin addict herself, because she seemed so hard and coarse.

She tells me to follow her and next I'm sitting in her cluttered office. As she sits at her desk she brushes a thick shock of hair away from her face and proceeds to tell me all about the clinic.

She relaxes a bit as she goes on about the deskmen, explaining how they help with the overall running of the rehab. I learn that the deskmen are very important because not only do they screen everyone who walks through the door, they also take the urine specimens from the patients and secure them in this big wooden box behind the desk. These are the specimens that the lab tests for licit and illicit drugs.

It was interesting to learn how the deskmen give the patients these orange preprinted labels which the patients then give to the dispensing nurses, who stick them on the bottles before hitting the machines that dispense the clear liquid methadone. (Each label features vital patient information, i.e., the patient's name, date of birth, dispensing date and milligram dosage.)

Well, at least this old harpy seems to know what she's talking about, I think, as I can't help but notice that her office is a mess. For starters, there are files scattered all over the place—on the floor, on the windowsill, on top of file cabinets—everywhere but on her desk. In addition, her wastebasket is filled to the brim with all sorts of shit, like soda cans and empty Styrofoam cups, and there's this fuckin' musty odor coming from where I don't know that makes me wanna puke.

This was a broad who liked to hear herself talk, and I was smart enough not to interrupt her. When she finally shuts up I just sit there like a moron, waiting for my cue. She stares at me like she's sizing me up, and when she's good and ready asks me if I have any questions. I ask her what the gist of the job is and she gives me the canned answer.

"Mr. Selkirk, methadone is a synthetic designed to satisfy the heroin addict's cr?

heroin. When properly administered it will also prevent or ease the symptoms of heroin withdrawal. Patients can live normal and productive lives while on a good methadone maintenance treatment program and can eventually become illicit drug free. Some patients successfully detox from methadone as well, and if we hire you your basic function will be to help the patients on your caseload. You will be required to develop the appropriate treatment care plans for your patients and help them make progress in their treatment. Does this sound like something that you'd like to do?"

I answered her with a firm "Yes", and since I desperately needed a job I made up this really good bullshit story about how I was oh, so interested in helping people. I wanted to convince her that I was serious about this endeavor, and to make her understand that I wasn't just another fly-by-night who would quit after a short time.

I recall saying that I wanted to make a difference, that a career as a substance abuse counselor was a calling and all sorts of other corny shit. For good measure I also pointed out that I was an inner-city guy from the East Village—a neighborhood with a notorious drug scene—and that I had a B.A. in sociology.

She listened without interruption and when I was done she told me to come in the next day, a Thursday, for my second interview with Jan Waters, the chief administrator. She explained that the clinic was closed from 12 to 2 on Tuesdays and Thursdays so that staff meetings could be held and so that other business could be taken care of too, such as job interviews.

I thanked her and said that I looked forward to the second interview. On my way out a jolt ran down my spine as I spotted Pamm on line waiting to get medicated. Our eyes met briefly as I kept moving, anxious to get the hell out of there.

8

Pamm had already warned me not to let anyone in on the fact that we knew each other, so I took the train straight home without waiting for her. By six o'clock I was comfortably nestled in my recliner, smoking a joint and watching the evening news.

At around seven or so she comes in and I'm anxious to tell her all about my day. The thing was, she didn't seem too interested in hearing about it, and this really pissed me off.

Sure, she feigned interest as I got into my story, but she didn't even ask me one fucking question. Instead, she simply went about her business and pretty much blew me off. Then, when she picked up the phone to make a call I lost my temper and snatched the receiver out of her hand.

"What the fuck is this? I'm not allowed to use the phone?" she asked plaintively.

"What the fuck is this?" I mimicked.

"You convince me to apply for a job at your clinic, I do, and then you decide you don't give a shit. Fuck you, Pamm."

"That's not true, Billy. I do wanna know all about your interview. It's just that I was having some second thoughts."

"What are you talking about?"

"Well, what if it doesn't work out? I'm afraid that you'll get mad at me and kick me out."

"Oh, c'mon. You should know by now that I'm not like that."

"Maybe I should, but I don't."

"Try not to be so insecure. I'm not about to throw you out—especially when you're trying to help me. Okay?"

"Awesome."

"You don't have to get sarcastic about it. Forget it."

"And you don't have to be such a sensitive asshole—just tell me what happened today and let's stop fighting."

"Do you really wanna know?"

"YES! If you work at the clinic we'll have something in common."

I described my day from start to finish and she laughed at my characterizations and impressions. When I was done I asked her if she thought I could cut the mustard.

"Do you want me to be polite and tell you that you'll do great and that you'll love the place, or do you want me to be honest?"

"I want ya to lie to me because ya think that I'm a big fat schmuck."

"Oh, don't get mad. Look Billy, I think that you have the balls to work there for a while, like maybe a year or so, but after that you'll probably burn out just like the rest of 'em. Maybe you'll even be able to line up a better job before you burn out. If they offer it to you, take it—we need the money."

"We?"

"That's right, 'We', because if you get evicted for not paying the rent, I also get evicted."

"True. Now what's the deal with Selma Hack?"

"OOH—I hate that ugly bitch—we all do. You better not let 'er scare you, because once she smells blood you're through."

"WOW! You really hate her. Whaddid she do to you?"

"Whaddid she do? I'll tell you what she did. She puts this fuckin' notice on the wall near the front desk in the lobby about housing referrals for patients, and when I go to see her about it she treats me like shit. Even though I made an appointment she makes me wait for over an hour. Then, when she finally sees me she acts like she doesn't wanna be bothered. She gives me all this crap about how I don't qualify for this or that and she was real nasty about it. She wouldn't shut up for a second and every time that I tried to ask her a question she blew me off and got even bitchier. She made me feel like a bug on the wall."

"Shit, Pamm, it's a shame that you hadda put up—"
"WAIT—I'M NOT FINISHED YET! After she rushed me outta her office I was so mad that I waited outside of the clinic after they closed the building, plotting to kick her ass."

"So what happened?"

"It was getting dark and I got tired of waiting so I left."

"Aah, you're better off. You woulda only got in big trouble."

"I know, I know. Still—it might've been worth it."

"Do you mind if I change the subject, Pamm?"

"No. Go right ahead."

"Good, because tomorrow I got my second interview with some lady named Jan Waters and maybe you can gimme some advice about her."

"Sure, Billy. Hmm. Well, the most important thing for you to know is that Jan has almost all the power, even though it's Dailey's clinic."

"Dailey? Who's Dailey?"

"Don't interrupt me—I'll tell you about him later."

"Okay."

"Ya see Selma runs the place when Jan's out of the office which is almost always, but Jan's the one who fires counselors and kicks patients out. Selma wishes she could, but Jan has the last word when it comes to who's hired, who's fired, which patients stay, and which patients go. Remember, Selma is only the assistant asshole—Jan's the head asshole. Jan is also mean and bossy and she can do whatever she wants. If you wanna keep your job you better not cross that black bitch."

"I didn't know she was black. Now who the hell is Dailey?"

"Oh yeah. Dailey's the fucker who actually owns the clinic. He's some kind of doctor, a psychiatrist, I think. All he wants to do is make money, otherwise he doesn't give a shit about the patients or anyone else.

Maybe things would be better if he cared, I dunno. I don't see how things could be any worse."

"Does the place really suck that much?"

"Hey look—I'm telling you how it is—I'm also telling you that you should take the fuckin' job and find out for yourself. What the fuck are you so afraid of anyway? If you don't like it you can always quit."

"I know, I know."

"Good. Now shut up. I'm tired of talking about all of this shit. Let's smoke summa my weed. This girl from the clinic who wants to hook up with me gave me two big joints, the cunt. She said that it's better than ordinary commercial."

"A girl from the clinic?"

"Yeah, so? Whaddya think—just because you're on a program you stop doing drugs? Please. Most of us still do drugs and almost all of us smoke pot. That's why the clinic's such a great place to make connections."

"I see."

We spent the rest of the evening smoking weed and vegetating, which was good because I needed to save my strength for tomorrow's interview with this Jan character. I went to bed early knowing that Pamm was right, and that I should simply take the job if it was offered. Like she said, I could always quit.

9

In spite of my misgivings, the next day I kept my appointment and I arrived at the clinic twenty minutes early. Once again the deskman brusquely ordered me to sit down, and at about ten minutes to noon he locked the clinic door. Several patients came by about five minutes later and he reluctantly let them in. After they got medicated and left he locked the door again, acting very put out. Any patient wishing to get medicated between noon and 2 p.m. would be out of luck.

I was starting to enjoy my wait, because at around a quarter after twelve somebody began banging on the solid steel door, infuriating Guy, the deskman. I was able to tell from the small black and white TV monitor that it was a skinny little white dude with a goatee and a buzz cut.

Watching him jump up and down, pounding on the door with his mouth agape, was like watching some manic cartoon character.

What made it even funnier was Guy's reaction. Boy, was he pissed. His fat face was contorted in rage and he was grinding his teeth, but by the time he started cursing out loud and pacing the lobby floor the banging stopped. What a poor imby, I thought—this jackass is about to have a brain hemorrhage over what? Sheesh. Relax dude, you'll find someone else to beat up later.

The near hour wait flew right by, and by the time that Colleen had me summoned in for my second interview I was feeling pretty good. She had me sit at her desk and we made some nice small talk while I waited for Jan Waters. Jan kept me waiting for another thirty minutes or so, but I didn't even care because I enjoyed talking to Colleen. Finally, this tall, thin, dark complected black woman marches in and Colleen introduces us.

What struck me first about Jan was that she seemed very normal—at least when compared to Selma. She wasn't ugly or pretty, she was simply a nondescript fortyish black professional female who had the crisp, cold aura of any other middle management type.

She wore bright red lipstick and had short straight hair. She seemed very blase and oozed self-importance. She stuck out her right hand and as I shook it she smiled politely. She had me follow her to her office and as soon as we entered she asked me to sit down. She left the office door wide open, which I found comforting because it made me feel less claustrophobic.

Before she began the interview she picked up the phone and made a personal call, the rude bitch. After she hung up she looked me straight in the eye and it was time to give me the third degree. Apparently Selma was the good cop; Jan the bad cop.

"Thank you for coming today, Mister——
Selman?"

"Uh, no, actually it's Selkirk, Billy Selkirk."

"Okay, Mister Selkirk—Billy. As you may have
guessed I'm a very, very busy woman so I don't have
a lot of time. You're here because you need a job and
I'm interviewing you because we need a counselor.
Correct?"

"Correct."

"I'm glad that we agree. Now to be honest, Billy,
I'd prefer to hire someone with experience, but since
we need someone right away I'm inclined to give you
a chance."

"Well, I'll certainly do my best to make the most
of that chance."

"Hold on—we don't just hire anyone. If I hire you
it will be based on the fact that I get a good impression
from you. True, Selma feels that you may have
something to offer, but now you have to sell me."

"I think I know what you mean Ms. Waters. I
wouldn't want you to hire the wrong person for the
job—the thing is, is that I don't think that I'm the
wrong person."

"So what makes you think that you're the right
person?"

"Well, for one thing I have a B.A. in sociology."

"Big deal. Almost anyone who's taken a few psych
or sociology courses thinks that they can do this. That
doesn't necessarily mean a thing."

"I can see your point, but I'm also a street-smart
inner-city guy from the East Village which means that
I've developed a certain intuition about people."

"I don't know what you're talking about."

"Okay, then to put it bluntly, since I live in a junky neighborhood I think that I'm better equipped for this job than some of the others who may apply."

"Very well put. Yes, I do get the sense that you won't fall apart the first time that some patient says 'boo.' But are you sure that you want the job? It's not easy work."

"Oh, I'm absolutely sure."

"Will you give me at least a year?"

"You have my word."

"All right then. I'll take a gamble on you. The position starts at 23K—not a lot for New York, but I'm giving you the opportunity to enter a new career field. We can discuss a raise in one year—if things work out. Major medical kicks in after three months and you're also entitled to vacation days and sick days. Colleen can fill you in on all that. The patients on the caseload you'll be taking over have gone way too long without a counselor, so I need you to start this coming Monday. Is that okay with you?"

"That'll be fine."

"Do you have any questions?"

"Uh, no. I just want to thank you for hiring me."

"You're welcome. Just be here 9 a.m. sharp Monday. See Colleen. Selma will train you and if I get a chance I'll touch bases with you sometime next week—just to see how you're doing."

We stood up and shook hands on it. As I walked out of her office I heard her pick up the phone and move on to something else. Hell, I was relieved; I had a job.

10

When I told Pamm that I was hired by Jan she was thrilled. We had dinner at a Cuban restaurant to celebrate that Thursday night, but for the greater part of the weekend I kept to myself. Pamm understood, realizing that I had to get it together for Monday. She was smart; she knew that she also had a lot riding on my new job at the clinic so she didn't mess with me that weekend.

Nevertheless, I could barely hold down a cup of black coffee on Monday morning, so I skipped breakfast and left for the clinic at 8 a.m. sharp, full of anxiety and very preoccupied. My apprehension was heightened by the fact that I hadn't worked at any job for almost a year, and going back to work after such a long time was for me akin to taking an ice water bath.

On the subway ride to Jackson Heights I strategized. I wanted to take full advantage of the fact that I would be coming to this place with a clean slate, and I promised myself that I'd do my best not to fuck it up. I even convinced myself that being a substance abuse counselor was a cool job with a certain cachet—heroin chic and all that.

I arrived at the clinic to find a huge throng of patients lined up by the side of the building, all waiting to get medicated. This crazy queue snaked all the way down to the corner, and you could bet your bottom dollar that the folks on it would never be mistaken for the crowd waiting to get into the Met.

It was a motley crew, ethnically and racially diverse, with a good mix of men and women. The majority of them appeared to be in their thirties and forties, and there was even a smattering of well-dressed professional types.

I dreaded having to cut through to the front of the line, but I had no choice. I got a few dirty looks as I pushed my way toward the front door, murmuring to the patients that I worked there. Fortunately, no one tried to stop me. When I finally got to the door I had to bang on it very hard, and after a couple of stressful minutes someone recognized me and they let me in.

I gave the big black guy at the desk my name and he nodded, so I went straight to the business office. I waited at the wooden half-door for a few seconds, and as soon as I caught Colleen's attention she opened the door. She invited me to sit down and she offered me coffee, but I declined, explaining that I was too nervous for coffee. She laughed at that and tried to put me at ease. She gave me some forms to fill out and when I was done I just sat there and tried to relax.

I watched as things got going. Monday morning
le and bustle. Counselors and other personnel
inside to punch in and to see Colleen, as patients

hovered over the wooden half-door with all sorts of requests and questions.

Phones rang, doors banged, office machines hummed and file cabinets were constantly being opened and slammed shut. The waiting room by the medical examining offices was SRO, and the corridor leading to the business office was also filled with restless patients and new intakes waiting to be admitted.

It was engrossing live theatre but soon Colleen showed me to my office, this drafty little cubicle tucked way inside the building's bowels. Trapped in the asshole, I was, but if I didn't like it, tough; I was new.

I sat down in this old gray padded swivel chair, took a deep breath and closed my eyes. I stayed this way until I got bored, and then I decided to take a walk around the building.

Strange digs. The front of the building wasn't bad because here the offices faced the street and there were windows and plenty of natural light. Some of these offices were even paneled. This was luxurious compared to my side. My part of the building was more like a high school gym divvied up into little sections. When some of the other workers started looking at me funny, I decided that it was time to go back to my hole.

I sat down again and began rummaging through the file cabinet where the patients' case histories were stored. I pulled out a few, placed them on my cheap metal desk and began reading. About halfway through the first file I heard a knock at the door. I figured that it was Selma or Colleen. Au contraire. I opened the door to find this big fat Jewish guy demanding to see a counselor—any counselor. Ah, my first encounter with a patient.

11

As I stood face to face with this ornery schlep I figured no big deal, just say hello and ask him what he wants. So I did just that, and invited him to sit down in the green metal folding chair that was stationed at the left side of my desk.

Unsmiling, he refused. Instead, he said that his name was Harvey Kaplan and he demanded to know why he was getting the runaround regarding his request for a reduced schedule. I didn't know what he was talking about but I wanted to help him.

"Mister Kaplan, lemme be honest. This is my very first day. Gimme a chance to get organized and I'll see what I can do."

"Look pal, I don't wanna hear any bullshit," he said, angrily shifting from one foot to the other, like he had a snake crawling up his ass.

"Well, Harvey, I don't know what to tell you. As soon as I see Selma I'll definitely tell her that you were here about your schedule. That's all that I can do point."

He gave me a baleful stare and stroked his grayish brown walrus mustache.

"Na-ah, fugeddaboutit. That bitch won't do shit. I've had it with this dump. I'm gonna go to the office to tell that blonde with the big tits and the big hair to get my papers together. I'm gonna transfer to this clinic in the city. Fuck this place."

"Are you sure?"

"YA DAMN RIGHT I'M SURE! Selma keeps tellin' me that she'll take care of it and nuthin' happens. I'm not some fuckin' welfare case—I'm a union baker. I'm twelve weeks clean and I'm supposed to be on a three day schedule. I've had it with this zoo."

Without another word he was gone. I was beginning to see what Jan meant when she said that she didn't need anyone who would fall apart right away, and I was happy that I didn't let that fat bastard rattle me. Still, I couldn't blame the guy for being ticked off if what he said was true. Who could?

After he left I lit up a cigarette, hoping that no one would complain. I found an amber glass ashtray in one of the desk drawers and I made myself feel right at home. When I was through with the Marb it was time for lunch, and after lunch I read a few patient case histories and coasted.

Selma hadn't had a chance to meet with me but I didn't care, I was just glad that my first day was over and done with and that I was still employed. I made a point of saying good night to Colleen, punched out, and split at precisely 5:05 p.m.

I was in a good mood when I got home and I gave Pamm a big hello as soon as I walked in, but she barely noticed me. She was too busy bullshitting on the phone with some girl named Dexi, whom she had mentioned in passing once or twice. I didn't mind, I only wanted to eat my dinner and have a few beers. It was back to the rat race tomorrow and any small talk with Pamm could wait.

12

I spent the first hour of my second day hiding in my office, reading the morning paper and drinking my take out coffee. At around ten Selma came by, fidgety but friendly. She sat down and after a few polite questions about how I was doing, began my indoctrination.

I was all ears as she pointed out that the key to the job was in learning how to effectively deal with the patients. She earnestly explained how most of them were manipulative, and how "getting over" was a big part of the junky subculture. She illustrated her point with several anecdotes and I took what she said at face value.

She told me how the nurses had to carefully watch the patients swallow their dosages, and said that the nurses even had to make them open their mouths after swallowing, so that there could be no doubt that their dosages were consumed. This was extremely t because of the phenomenon known as eth."

I learned that there was a thriving market for methadone as an illicit drug, and that there were those patients who would hold it in their mouths, spit it out into some sort of container as soon as they left the clinic, and sell it. Then, they would use the proceeds from this cunning endeavor to buy recreational drugs.

She taught me all about dosage levels and urine profiles and went into the whole concept of reduced schedules. A reduced schedule was a privilege that a patient had to earn. Simply put, patients who worked the program could be presented by their counselors at the regular weekly meetings to be considered for this benefit.

For example, unless he worked or was in school, a new patient would start out on a six day a week schedule, as the clinic was closed on Sunday. After twelve consecutive weeks of illicit drug free urine toxicity results, he could earn a day off and get another take home bottle. After six months of clean urines, if a patient worked and could prove it, he could qualify for the thrice weekly plan. (Occasionally, students could also qualify.) Reduced schedules varied, but each patient had a chance to earn their "days."

This was no easy task because most patients want to get high, methadone or not. The ones that do succeed are the exceptions, so it's easy to understand why a poor slob like Kaplan was so frustrated and antagonistic.

Very few patients ever earned reduced schedules of once or twice a week. A patient had to be clean for two straight years for the twice a week job and three straight years for the once-a-weeker. But, no matter how good your tox sheet looked, if you weren't in school o work, with rare exception, you'd never do better than five days.

From what I was told this was state law, the theory being that indolent patients need structure, and reporting to a clinic five to seven days a week would help turn them into more responsible citizens.

It is significant to note that many of the patients on 1x, 2x, and 3x schedules were being maintained on low and ridiculously low dosages. One guy on my caseload came in once a week, was on five milligrams and worked as a computer repair technician; another patient, this lady who worked for the Post Office, came in twice a week and was on ten milligrams. Patients like these were simply afraid of doing the total detox.

Of course, critics of methadone maintenance treatment have rightfully pointed out that methadone was never meant to be a way of life, but that's exactly the way it is for so many.

Back in the late sixties, before the advent of the clinic, the lobbyists and their experts painted this rosy picture of methadone as a panacea. Society would benefit profoundly, they theorized, as patients would have their physical need for dope satiated, and after a reasonable period would be weaned off of methadone.

The painful truth is that very few patients prevail this way, that many have been on this drug for years and years, and that a good number of them will undoubtedly die on it.

13

During that first week, Selma did a thorough job of training me. She repeatedly stressed that everything between counselor and patient had to be kept on the up and up, and bluntly told me to avoid any questionable contact with the patients, especially the women.

With somber relish, she related how the counselor who had my caseload before me, some tool named Frank Picone, had gotten fired for having sex with one of his female patients. This schmuck had only been on the staff for a few months when the girl squealed, resulting in his termination.

As Selma told it, Picone and his paramour had this quid pro quo going, the idea being that in exchange for blow jobs in his office, he would pull some strings and reward her with a reduced schedule. He promised her this even though she hadn't had a clean urine during her entire 28 month tenure.

Naturally, when the girl had finally realized that she'd been sucking his cock in vain, the jig was up. Selma also made it quite clear that there was a clinic "chain of command." She said that I was to go to her and her alone with any questions or concerns, and strongly advised me against seeking counsel elsewhere. This was a little too much. It was only my second day, but she was getting on my nerves and I felt like asking her if she wanted my size 11 boot up her ass.

After lunch I had the pleasure of attending my first clinic meeting. We were all seated at this long rectangular table, four counselors at each side, with Selma sitting by herself up front. I sat there awkwardly as she started things off, introducing me to the staff. She pointedly mentioned that the clinic would be fully staffed as soon as one more counselor was hired, and almost everyone nodded in approval.

I couldn't help but notice that this was no lily white male sanctuary. Only three of the eight counselors present were men, and out of the whole group there were four whites, one hispanic, and three blacks.

After some small talk with one of the women, Selma got down to business.

"Okay everyone, does anyone have any presentations?" she asked.

Immediately, a short, squat black girl in her early twenties stood up.

"Yes Selma, I have a presentation today. I wanna present Daysi Quinones."

I learned that this counselor's name was Sabrina Clark and that she was considered to be a "senior counselor", having been with the clinic for more than a year.

"Daysi's been with the clinic for one year and two months. The last time I presented her she was rejected because she had a dirty urine. It's been twelve weeks since that presentation and she's been clean since then. I called up the lab today and they said that the supervised urine that I took on her last Friday was meth only," she said.

Sabrina continued. "Daysi's on public assistance and food stamps and she has three kids, ages four, six and ten. She's single and she says that she don't have the time to take vocational training. She wants to go from six to three days but I told her that the best we can do is five, unless she gets a job or goes to school."

Sabrina passed around this sheet that had this grid which showed the results of this patient's last twelve urine tests. Selma asked the group if there were any objections, and after a minimal amount of discussion Daysi was awarded a five day schedule. Of course, if she screwed up just once over the next twelve weeks she'd go right back to six.

There were several other presentations and a few announcements. Then, before she adjourned the meeting, Selma took count of each counselor's caseload and at the end of the meeting she handed me three new shiny pink files. These were my new patients and as we walked out of the room together, Selma informed me that I would soon be doing intakes.

An intake was just that; the admission or taking in of a patient. Some of these people were new to the clinic but many were readmissions, and most of those who were first timers at Jackson Heights had previously been patients at other methadone clinics. Very few patients were methadone virgins.

To do an intake a counselor had to set up a new patient file, meaning that he had to do a psycho-social history. A psycho-social history meant that the counselor would interview the prospective patient by sticking to the questions on the psycho-social history form. The counselor would ask the questions and fill out the questionnaire, paraphrasing the patient's responses.

After the interview the counselor would check the patient's arms and hands for needle marks, and after that the patient would be brought to the doctor or physician's assistant for the physical. Patients would be warehoused in the waiting room until the MD or PA was ready, and as a part of the exam, urine and blood specimens would be taken.

When the patient was finished with the doctor, the counselor would make the arrangements for a supervised urine. Sometimes the intake counselor would supervise the patient urinating into the small plastic bottle (which would go to the lab), but not always. Mainly it depended on the new patient's gender; a male counselor could only supervise males and vice versa. Counselors worked with each other when it came to admissions, and as a rule intakes usually came off with few problems.

The last step in the process was when the counselor took the patient's picture, with this special camera that made a print with four passport sized photos. The counselor would use two of these Polaroid photos for the patient's ID cards; one card would go to the patient and one would go to the deskman, who would file it ˡphabetically. The extra photos would either go in the garbage or be stapled to the patient's file; it didn't matter.

What did matter was that the patient's supervised intake specimen had to test positive for opiates; obviously a patient could not be admitted otherwise. In my experience at the clinic this was never a problem and it was difficult to imagine how it could be. To the contrary, new admissions usually tested positive for several drugs in addition to heroin, most commonly cocaine, benzodiazepines, and alcohol.

Although marijuana was considered an illicit drug, it was an open secret to everyone that the lab never tested for it because the clinic didn't require it. From what I had heard a tox screen for pot was not cost efficient, so it was to hell with it. As far as I was concerned, as a pot smoker, a counselor, and a human being, this was great.

If they tested for pot it would only make the plight of these people much more difficult and if you have to ask why...

I began to get to know some of the other counselors and I learned some of the finer points of this art by watching them. I was trained to look not just for needle marks, but also for scars. Scars could mean that the patient was a self-mutilator, and/or had a history of suicide attempts. If anything like this was suspected, it would be duly noted. At minimum, old needle marks provided a visual history of the patient's IV drug use.

The other counselors also told me all about "stops." A stop was an order placed by a counselor or some other person in authority that popped up on the when the dispensing nurse saw the patient.

meant that said patient would have to see the person who placed the stop before he could get medicated.

Most of the stops were put there by the counselors regarding treatment issues, but stops could also be ordered by the administration for a variety of reasons. If a patient was stopped by Colleen, for instance, it was usually because their account was in arrears.

This system generally worked pretty well, although patients sometimes tried to get around it. Let's say that a counselor had a stop on—the patient could leave the nurses' station for a few minutes and then come back, giving the nurse some bullshit story about how the counselor wasn't in. Occasionally patients could get over this way but most patients complied, realizing that the counselor would just keep putting the stops on until they met. Man, how patients hated to be stopped.

By the middle of my second week I was ready to rumble, despite the fact that I didn't know what I was doing.

The first patients that I stopped were the ones with the worst illicit drug profiles, and such a patient was Doreen McQueen. Doreen was 23, but she looked like an old forty. In fact, she reminded me of an old Irish washerwoman, like from the cartoons. Of medium build, she was sallow, gaunt, and irritable.

From the moment that we met it was like, "Great, here's another clueless asshole who's out to hassle me." She asked me to lift the stop and I asked her to sit down. She did. She was very uncommunicative, despite my best efforts to be charming. For a second I thought about my predecessor, Picone, and how he must have been pretty horny to get it on with any of these skanks.

Doreen didn't know or care that I was actually sympathetic towards her and her plight. A high school drop out at age 16, her Irish/Italian Catholic parents had seen fit to throw her out of the house at around the same time that she had left school. Shortly thereafter she had gotten involved with this Dominican guy who was by now ancient history, but during their fling he had managed to knock her up and her biracial daughter was now almost four.

Next to a lot of these losers she didn't look so bad. True, she had a record for shoplifting, discon, and prostitution, but so what? If she could conquer her multiple addictions and put her mind to it she could probably make it, because relatively speaking she wasn't all that fucked up.

Thanks to the New York City Department of Social Services she had a place to live and received a small monthly welfare check, and due to the courtesy of the federal government she was on food stamps, AFDC, and medicaid. She was doing better than many of the working poor, and her daddy, who had a few connections via his long tenure as a city cop, pulled some strings to get her into one of the better city housing projects.

She lived in a great Manhattan neighborhood that people like me only dreamed about, near York and 86th Street, and in a year or so her daughter could attend a good local public school.

I offered her a Marlboro, which she snatched from me, and I lit her cigarette with mine. I began our introductory session by reminding her that she hadn't seen a counselor for a long time, and that according to the rules, each patient was supposed to meet with his or her counselor once a week.

She didn't respond verbally, she only shrugged and looked bored. For a few uncomfortable moments we both just sat there, but then she put out the cigarette, rubbed her nose, and flatly asked me to lift the stop. Instead, I began my lecture.

"You know Doreen, I'd like to present you for a reduced schedule someday, but your urines have been dirty for like the last twenty weeks in a row. You're already up to seventy milligrams, but very soon we're gonna have to go to the doctor for a dosage increase to eighty milligrams. Perhaps that would help."

Again, no response. She just looks at me funny, as if to say, "Who the fuck are you to tell me what to do?" I offered her another cigarette which she accepted, and made a little small talk. It didn't work. She looked at her feet, looked at the wall, and when she couldn't ignore me any longer, looked at me. Then, she declared that she was in a rush and demanded that I lift the stop.

What could I do? I told her that we'd be meeting again, called the nurses' station and had the stop lifted. She darted out of my office, and as soon as she was gone I breathed a sigh of relief and wondered if I was cut out for this sort of thing.

14

I had completed my second full week at work and I was feeling good. I was back in the game—I had a job, an apartment in one of the trendiest sections of Manhattan, and I didn't have any big problems.

There was one thing, though, that was bugging me—Pamm. I mean this junky bitch princess had a pretty good deal going since she latched on to me. Free room and board, free phone service, free beer, and even free cable. Nice.

So, what was I getting back in return? Snotty bullshit—and this was from someone who would still be living with the rats if it wasn't for me. The little bitch would hardly even talk to me, she would just nod and mumble whenever I tried to make friendly conversation. I was feeling used and I resented it.

This cunt from the squats had another thing coming if she thought that I was gonna be ignored. No way. I was so nice to her—I never touched her and she had carte blanche around my place, yet she acts like I'm annoying her whenever I say hello. What kind of crap was this?

Another thing that was pissing me off about her was that other cunt, Dexi. Almost every day after work I would spot those two little whores loitering on St. Mark's, near this fleabag hotel, panhandling.

What is with this skinny bitch? If she can hassle strangers for change she can work, and I bet that she and Dexi are busy having sex with each other in my apartment while I'm out there breaking my ass, working. She thinks she owns the joint.

Okay, so I'll toss her ass out. Oh, really. For what? For hurting my feelings? When she moved in she wasn't holding a gun to my head—I let her move in. Jesus Christ, I may be a schmuck for letting her con her way in here with that sob story, but I don't wanna be a prick, too. Unless she pulls some seriously wicked shit, I'm stuck with her. Sigh.

Days and nights went by and we barely said two words to each other, but all that changed one fateful Friday evening.

Exhausted and stressed out after a particularly difficult work week, I went to bed at about midnight, hoping that a good night's sleep would clear my head.

Fat chance. The clock said 3:17 when I was awakened by a loud thud. I staggered out of bed, threw on a pair of shorts and opened my bedroom door very slowly, as my bleary blue eyes needed time to adjust to the light. I walked past the kitchen and into the living room, afraid of what I might find.

What I found was a very stoned Pamm and a very stoned Dexi sitting on the futon, yogi style, smoking a joint. They had knocked down my favorite beer mug and broken it. It was an antique, one of those old style heavy glass mugs that you used to find in all the Irish bars, the bars where the longshoremen and construction workers drank.

I was pissed, really pissed. They had busted the handle off and they didn't seem to know or care. They were oblivious to me and my mug, but I was about to change that.

First, I shut off the stereo. They had this crazy thumping techno music on and it wasn't helping any. Then, I walked over to Pamm and grabbed her by the hair.

"OWW!—WHAT THE FUCK ARE YOU DOING?" she shrieked.

"GETTING YOUR ATTENTION!" I shouted back.

"LOOK, YOU FUCKERS WOKE ME UP AND BUSTED MY FAVORITE BEER MUG, SO I'M NOT IN SUCH A GREAT MOOD—OKAY?"

"I didn't break your mug—Dexi did. She knocked it over when she was reaching for—"

"That's not the point Pamm. The point is that this is my place and you don't seem to give a shit about that. If you think that you can—"

"Oh, shuddup you fat dork. We were only goofing around," Dexi chimed in, totally wasted.

"Oh, hello. I don't believe we've met. My name is Billy. You must be Dexi. Is that right?"

"Yeah, that's right."

"Well, Dexi, if you don't get your skinny little white trash piece a shit ass outta here in like ten seconds, I'm throwing you out."

"Fuck you."

"FUCK ME? WELL FUCK YOU TOO!"

She didn't know what hit her, as I grabbed her by the waist of her filthy jeans and proceeded to toss her butt out.

"WHADDA YA DOIN'? GETCHA HANDS OFFA ME YOU MUTHAFUCKA! OWW! PAMM, HELP ME! OWW!" she screamed, as I shoved her into the hall and slammed the door in her face.

Seconds later she was back, banging the door down, demanding her things. I had Pamm hand me her ratty leather motorcycle jacket and her crumpled pack of Camels. I put the Camels in one of the pockets and I chucked the jacket out the living room window. It landed on the sidewalk, next to one of the building's metal garbage cans.

"LISTEN, YOU BITCH—IF YOU WANT YOUR SHIT YOU BETTER RUN OUTSIDE BECAUSE I JUST THREW YOUR CRAP OUT THE WINDOW! SOME BUM EVEN WORSE THAN YOU IS GONNA STEAL IT!"

Pamm and I both laughed hysterically as she clomped down the stairs, and we almost pissed in our pants as we watched her scurry out of the building and pick up her jacket. We sat by the living room window as she made tracks down 7th Street, and as soon as she disappeared I got up and went back to bed.

When I woke up a few hours later Pamm was sleeping in my blue corduroy recliner, all splayed out, clad only in pink panties and a thin T-shirt. If I had fucked her right there she wouldn't have even known it, but I had better things to do.

I took a shower, ate breakfast, and got dressed. It was only 12:30 and it was a nice, crisp autumn Saturday. The sun was shining, the birds were singing, and I just wanted to get out for a while.

Then, just as I was about to leave, Pamm got up. She asked me where I was going. I told her that it was none of her fuckin' business, and as she began to mumble something about how she needed gum and cigarettes, I nonchalantly walked out. Let her get off her ass and buy her own gum and cigarettes, I thought, as I ignored her.

I decided to take a long walk out to the West Village—the area around West 3rd Street and 7th Avenue South. On my way down there I stopped off at this deli near 8th Avenue and Christopher Street. I bought a shrimp salad sandwich on a kaiser roll and a large light coffee—no sugar.

I ate my lunch in this little park in the heart of gay Greenwich Village and sat by the statues of the two gay couples. It was nice to be out of my grungy neighborhood for a change. There were trees in full autumn bloom everywhere, the air smelled sweet, and obviously a finer class of people lived here.

After I finished my sandwich I just sat around and mellowed out. What a tranquil place to be, I mused; besides the trees there's all of this shrubbery and nature. No rats in these parts, just squirrels and birds and fine architecture. I sighed and wished that I made the kind of dough that could net me a decent one bedroom here.

Yeah, right. I lingered until I got bored and then I got up and headed back towards alphabetland.

I took my sweet time, stopping off in several bookstores and record shops as I daydreamed about things. By the time that I got back to the 'hood it was almost dark and I was getting hungry again. I was in a good mood when I opened the door to my apartment, but a surly Pamm greeted me as soon as I walked in.

"Did you have a nice day, asshole?" she asked, her eyes shooting daggers and her voice cold and vicious.

"Yes I did, Pamm. Too bad you couldn't join me," I laughed.

"Ya know, ya didn't havta be so mean ta Dexi last night and ya coulda waited for me today."

"What the hell are you complaining about? You were rolling on the floor laughin' when I threw her out."

"Well, I couldn't help it. I still think you were way harsh."

"Tough."

"Fuck you, Billy."

"Fuck you too, Pamm. Maybe it's time you considered moving outta here if you're so ticked off. I don't fuckin' need ya—especially with your attitude."

To my amazement she shut up. Good. Too damn bad if I hurt her delicate feelings. Yeah, yeah, yeah, I understood that she was just a dumb girl, but I had to draw the line somewhere, and I was fed up with her anyway. Maybe she didn't know it, but she was on probation, and if she didn't get her shit together her days with me were numbered.

15

I was happy to be back at work on Monday after all of the nonsense that had taken place over the weekend. This joy was short-lived, however, as I was soon jolted back to reality by several loud raps. I opened the door to find this rawboned, Slavic looking creep frothing at the mouth, apparently in a state of apoplexy over what I didn't know.

Before he had a chance to say anything I asked him to step into my little office and he did, but he refused to sit down.

If he wasn't gonna sit I wasn't gonna sit, so there we both stood, glaring at each other.

"Who are you and what do you want?" I asked.

"My name's Lewicki, and I want my Saturday back."

"I've seen your chart Lewicki, but I never raised your schedule."

"Then who the fuck did?"

"I don't know. Sit down and I'll try to find out."

We both took our seats and I pulled out his urine grid. He was a new readmit and although his first three urines were dirty, by rights he still had another week to get his shit together. I called the office and I asked Colleen what his current dosage was and she said that he was on 40 milligrams. It turned out that he had recently asked the PA for a dosage increase, which was cool, and he had given his last urine on Friday, only three days earlier.

During my investigation Lewicki was getting antsy. He was acting like a jerk and making things more difficult.

"Look, Mr. Lewicki, I'm doing the best that I can. Lemme call the lab and see how your last tox came out."

"YOU DON'T UNDERSTAND! I NEED MY WEEKENDS OFF SO I CAN WORK!" he yelled.

"YA KNOW, I'M GETTIN' SICK OF PEOPLE TELLIN' ME THAT I DON'T UNDERSTAND. IF I DIDN'T UNDERSTAND I'D CALL THE DESK AND HAVE SECURITY THROW YOU OUTTA MY OFFICE. LET ME DO MY JOB!" I shouted back.

Surprised by my outburst, he shut up. I called the lab and they told me that his last urine was clean. I put the urine book away, pulled out a cigarette, lit it up and also offered one to him. He accepted.

"Mr. Lewicki, the good news is that your last urine was clean, so now I can work on getting you your day back. In the meantime, see me once a week, and don't do any illicits."

"Yeah, great. Now would ya mind tellin' me— WHO THE FUCK RAISED MY SCHEDULE?"

"I don't know. What difference does it make? The main thing is for me to get you your Saturday back and then for you to follow our treatment care plan."

"Listen, you—I make my living installing drywall, I work on Saturdays and I don't wanna hear any bullshit. Would you do me a favor and get me my day back? PLEEZE?"

I pondered the question, and since he was right, I had to do something. His nasty attitude was besides the point. I called Colleen to find out who put in the order and she informed me that it was Selma, as if I didn't know. I took a deep breath and called the bitch. Unfortunately, she picked up on the second ring. Great. She's always so elusive and now she's in. Today's my lucky day.

"Selma, good morning, this is Billy. I have a patient here named James Lewicki. He's very upset because you upped his pickup schedule from five to six days. His first three urines were dirty but his last one was clean—I just checked with the lab. I guess that there's some sort of mix-up. What do we do?"

"Is he in your office?"

"He's sitting right here."

"You're not supposed to discuss something like this while the patient is in your office listening," she said, her voice brittle.

"Okay, sorry. All I know is that he's angry and he wants his day restored."

"I have a patient in my office right now with much bigger problems than Lewicki," she seethed.

"I'm just trying to follow clinic policy and deal with this patient, Selma. Sorry, but I don't understand this."

"DON'T TALK TO ME IN THAT TONE OF VOICE!" she raged.

Wow, I thought, she's nuts.

"Well, what do I do?" I asked flatly.

"TAKE IT TO THE ADMINISTRATION!" she bellowed, hanging up on me.

I was worn out. I told Lewicki to follow me and we both went to see Jan. I told her the story and when I was done I got the impression that Selma had pulled this kind of shit before.

Jan was curt and blase as she called the lab to verify everything that I had already verified, restoring Lewicki's day and dismissing us both with the back of her hand in one fell swoop. Thanks, Jan.

Mission accomplished. Lewicki got his day back and he even patted me on the back and shook my hand. Boy, what a nice creep. I felt a twinge of smug satisfaction as he walked away, but by the time that I got back to my office I was beginning to feel sorry for myself. What bothered me was everybody's hostility.

I mean first I get all of this shit from the patient for something that he thinks I did, then I get even worse shit from the bitch who started the whole thing, and finally, when I go to the boss for help she treats me like a pest. Not only that, but to top it off, I'm also getting sucked into the office politics of this dump. Jesus.

Alas, I was clueless no more. Everybody hates this fuckin' place and everybody hates Selma and now I know why, but what good does it do me? I need the steady income and I got no other prospects so I'm stuck here and I better make it work.

On the train ride home that night I tried to read the paper but that was impossible because I had a headache. A bad headache. I felt like taking my right thumb and sticking it into my right eye, the headache's epicenter. So this is what I get for taking an asshole job in an asshole place—a splitting headache, undoubtedly the first of many more to come.

16

Despite a few dirty looks from Selma, the next couple of weeks turned out to be pretty routine, as I continued my on the job training. I did my intakes, entered the tox results in the urine book, and worked very hard to bring all of my charts up to date. It was during this period that I did a lot of "ghostwriting", as it's known in the trade.

Selma let me in on this phenomenon and taught me how to do it.

She explained that for a clinic to pass muster with state auditors, each patient's file had to be complete and current, with no gaps. Thus, a new counselor had to connect the dots during those periods when the patients on his caseload were in-between counselors, meaning that he had to fabricate in writing what went on during counseling sessions that had never actually taken place.

As corrupt as it may seem, it was really no big deal. To fill in the gaps the counselor would simply make up dates and jot down some very short notes, something like: "Met with patient today to discuss his TCP (treatment care plan). Went over all important issues and emphasized to patient the importance of seeing counselor on a weekly basis."

Every counselor had to fabricate from time to time, and since passing state audits was paramount as far as the administration of any methadone clinic was concerned, this *WAS* the job. Every clinic was audited at least once a year, so if a counselor kept good charts his bosses would be very happy with him.

In an ideal system none of this bullshit would be tolerated, but the system was far from ideal. Ghostwriting was a necessary evil, because without it clinics could be shut down by state auditors.

As far as I was concerned, the real evil was the state's insistence on comprehensive paperwork instead of comprehensive treatment. Obviously, this was a system in dire need of reform.

The upshot was that too many counselors cruised on their paperwork, and the patients of these counselors suffered for it.

Methadone treatment was always supposed to be about more than just dispensing a synthetic opiate; however, if the truth be told, that's pretty much *ALL* that it's about. Who cares, right? As long as the junkies aren't busy robbing us blind because they're on the program everybody's happy. Right? Not exactly.

In fact, methadone maintenance treatment is held in dubious regard by many of the professionals who work in the addiction recovery field. The reason for this is very clear-cut—methadone in and of itse extremely addictive drug.

The bottom line is that methadone clinics in New York City provide little more than methadone. Sure, at Jackson Heights there was always talk of this service and that service, but that's mostly all it was, talk.

For example, the clinic administration was proud of the fact that they offered in-clinic support groups. True, once in a while some counselor would run some kind of a support group at Selma's behest, but every fucking group that was ever offered would mysteriously dissipate after only a few sessions. Every group.

The way it worked was that during one of the regularly scheduled meetings in the conference room, Selma would ask if anyone would be willing to run, let's say, a group for HIV patients. Everyone would look at everyone for a few moments, some counselor would inevitably volunteer, and now there was this new support group.

Before you knew it, someone would put up posters, staff members would spread the word, and if enough interest was generated, patients would appear at the designated time.

I would even bet that the patients who attended these groups benefited from them and that these group sessions had considerable therapeutic value, so the groups were a good thing. The problem was that the patients couldn't count on the counselors who ran them to keep them going.

One of the most pathetic sights you would ever see in the clinic was some meek, bedraggled patient waiting by the conference room, only to be told that there wouldn't be a group today because of this, that, or the other thing. Either have the goddamn groups or don't have 'em, but stop doing things so half-assed. It simply was not right.

There was also a job and vocational placement service handled by Selma that consisted of little more than her postings of last Sunday's classified ads on her office door. To be fair, occasionally she could be very helpful in placing a patient in a job or training program, but this was rare.

The reason that this service wasn't working was because seeing Selma was just too much of a hassle for most of the patients. She was always busy with some crisis or another and any appointment meant at least an hour's wait.

Then, when the patient finally managed to see the great lady, the patient would more often than not get turned off by her imperious, condescending manner. In other words, she made them feel like shit. Consequently, only the most determined got anywhere, and since you don't find too many of these types in methadone clinics, the jobs program sucked.

Since most of these souls were on Medicaid, New York State picked up the tab for the majority of the patients, so Dailey never had to worry about his cash cow crapping out and had little incentive to improve clinic services.

Dailey had it made. Take roughly 700 patients, multiply that number by the weekly fee (which was in the area of fifty dollars), times that amount by 52, and you got yourself a multi-million dollar business. Year, after year, after year.

From time to time when the census would to under 700, Dailey would get a little edgy, so behest, during one of the regular meetings Selma would make an issue out of it. She would ask us counselors why the patients were leaving, just to see what we would say. She knew why.

Some left because they were flighty fly-by-nights, some got busted, some croaked, and some (like Harvey Kaplan) transferred because they didn't like the way that they were being treated.

The reasons varied, but Dailey didn't have much to worry about. Selma had a good time with us by hinting that if the census didn't pick up counselors could get laid off, but it was just blather.

Business always got better, especially during the winter, on account of the fact that these characters needed a safe harbor when it got cold. Who wants to run around making connections when it's freezing?

The bottom line was that this was New York, the junky capital of the world, a place where there would always be a never-ending supply of patients.

17

That infamous Saturday of Dexi and the broken beer mug and Pamm calling me an asshole and me telling her that I didn't fuckin' need 'er, had turned out to be our watershed.

For now anyway, everything was very free and easy, we got along fine and I enjoyed having her. She was doing her best to behave herself and I tried not to hassle her.

I even managed to keep my mouth shut when she shot up at the kitchen table, right in front of me. I mean it wasn't like she made me watch, it was more like this is my place too, I'm a junky, and this is what junkies do.

I saw how she cooked up the bags in a spoon, drew up the dope into a syringe, tied off her arm and injected herself. Ten minutes later she was nodding out on the futon.

What could I do about it? I knew that this was a part of the deal when she moved in with me, and that she would stop only when she wanted to stop and that could be never. From time to time I'd mumble something to her about a meth dosage increase, but other than that I minded my own business.

Being a pothead and a drinker myself, I was in no position to judge her and tell her what to do. Not only that, but ever since we started sleeping together the dynamics of our relationship had changed, and I didn't want to rock the boat.

And what a funky little relationship it was. One night she "accidentally" walks in on me while I'm in the bathroom jerking off, and ever since then we're getting it on all the time.

Pamm had a tight, exciting pussy and I was all too happy to let her orchestrate this latest turn of events. Man, was she fine. I had 'er upside down, right side up, over me and under me. I tossed 'er around like a rag doll and she squeezed my balls 'til I screamed. Tongues and fingers went everywhere and almost nothing was taboo. We had good, hot sex and things would never be the same. Ooh…Ahh…

Who knew what the future would bring and who cared?

18

There was this one patient on my caseload, this young Puerto Rican guy, Hector Ortiz, who had absolutely no interest in becoming illicit drug free. He was a lowlife and a ne'er-do-well, but I liked him because he didn't try to bullshit me.

He had to see me after I put a stop on, and right from the start I got the feeling that this was a dude who knew the game. A long time methadone patient, he had been in and out of various clinics and rehabs over the years, and he let me know right off the bat that he wasn't gonna change.

"Okay. I'm here. So whatcha want?"

"Well, first I wanna tell you that you should see me if you need anything—ya know, like dosage increases, reinstatement if you miss a day—ya know, just about anything clinic related."

"Good."

"I also wanted to tell you that on ninety milligrams you're supposed to have clean urines and since your urines are always dirty I havta tell Selma, who has to tell Dailey, who then will most likely raise you to one hundred milligrams, the highest dosage permitted by state law. He may even stop you himself. He might read you the riot act and tell you that if you don't get your shit together he's gonna bounce your ass outta here."

"So? I can always go to another clinic."

"True, but wouldn't that be a hassle?"

"I can deal with it."

"Okay, but just out of curiosity, do you really wanna be on dope forever?"

"It's a life."

"Yeah, but you must be doing ten bags a day."

"Whaddya expect? I'm on methadone—how else can I feel the heroin?"

"Yeah, but—"

"Yeah, but what? C'mon, man, I just like gettin' high."

"All right—I get the point. I'll lift the stop. You can go get medicated."

" 'Bye."

So, put that in all the textbooks, because in many cases it's as simple as that—some patients just like getting high.

19

It was getting cold outside. Winter was here and a New York winter means fear and despair for most who live on the margins. Some will even die. It's also a busy time of the year at methadone clinics throughout the city, as the last thing that a junky needs to face is involuntary heroin withdrawal when it's 10 degrees outside with a wind chill factor of minus 30.

As the temperatures plummeted and the weather grew increasingly miserable, Pamm turned up the heat on me. She wanted me to do something that I was totally against. She wanted me to let her friend Dexi live with us.

The first time that she asked me I looked at her like she was crazy and I didn't even bother to answer. She waited a day and then asked me again. This time I simply said no and changed the subject. And then she asked me again and again and again, telling me about how she and Dexi were lovers, and how she loved me too, and how we could all be a family. She w on about how great it would be if I would only give Dexi a chance.

Every night after I came home from work she would start in on me, saying that Dexi didn't have anyplace to live and how she was gonna freeze to death. When I told her that I didn't give a rat's ass, she tried to sweeten the deal by telling me how sure she was that Dexi would have sex with me and how we could have threesomes.

No way Pamm. But whyyyy? Because she gives me the creeps. There's something about her that ain't quite right. Yeah, well, there's something about you that ain't quite right, Billy, you fat asshole. Shut up Pamm—it's my place and I don't want her here and that's that. Dork. Whore. You better shut up Billy. No, you shut up…No, you shuddup…You shut up…No, you shut up…

Oh, c'mon Billy. You c'mon, Pamm. Why should I give a shit if that little guttersnipe lives or dies? Why? Because I love her, Billy.

Sorry, Pamm but your girlfriend gives me the creeps and the answer is no. NO! NO! NO! NO! NO!

Surprisingly, after I had made it clear for the last time that I wanted no part of this, Pamm finally shut up. She didn't even pout. Even more surprisingly, one night after work I came home to find Dexi sleeping on the futon while Pamm was busy cooking spaghetti. Too bad Bill, Dexi's living with us whether you like it or not. So there.

Oh sure, I could have had a fit and tossed the bitch out, but Pamm and I had been doing so well together, and if I had done that then everything would have been ruined. So Dexi was here—at least for now.

Little by little I got to know Dexi. Guess what, Billy, my real name is Dawn and I'm from West Virginia. I came to New York because my family is trailer trash and I hate West Virginia. Someone told me that for New York Dexi sounds a lot cooler than Dawn, so I changed my name. Listen, I'm sorry I dissed you that night but I know that we can all be friends and have a lotta fun. Okay? Yeah, great.

So what could I do? At least the skinny little white trash wench was trying to be polite. Just the same, I didn't like anything about this set up, and even though I tried to make the best of it she still gave me the creeps.

With her milky white skin, short shaggy platinum blonde hair, thin bluish lips and pale blue eyes, I reckon that she must have been of hillbilly descent and that her parents were first cousins—or worse.

Still, she did have a certain raw charm. For one thing, she really wasn't all that unattractive. Her tits were small and firm and bouncy (just the way I like 'em), her ass was round and tight, and she was very thin and petite. She was a girl, I'll give her that.

I also had to give her credit for making Pamm happy, and it was nice to see the two girls laughing and giggling. One night, in fact, I was so taken by their mirth that I treated us all to dinner at the Odessa.

They both bubbled over that night, especially Dexi, who was in dire need of a good meal. The poor thing had been living on street drugs and cigarettes, so her overanxiousness was understandable.

We had an early five o'clock supper and Dexi did her best to be amusing, peppering me with all sorts of silly questions and cracking jokes about other diners in the restaurant, pointing them out and making fun of them. She was so stupid she was funny, and she actually got me to laugh, which was no small accomplishment.

We had a long, leisurely dinner, with the two chippies pinching and touching each other, taking their time, and ordering lots and lots of food. In short, we had a rowdy good time.

What a strange and wonderful evening. Later, after we had arrived back at the apartment, Pamm and Dexi shot up dope together and shortly afterwards they were both nodding out on my big queen-sized bed. They lay side by side like two little girls, exhausted after a day of fun and games. I let them be, wondering if theirs wasn't the better way.

20

It only took a few days before Pamm and Dexi started getting sick of each other, and the laughing and giggling became screaming and yelling. Since I was at work during the day I never caught much of it, but the other tenants in the building sure as hell did. People in the building were complaining to the super, and now the super was complaining to me.

According to him there wasn't a curse word that these girls didn't know, and he bluntly told me in his Dominican accent that if they didn't cool it he was going to tell the owner to evict us. He wasn't kidding, either, so I slipped him a sawbuck and pleaded with him to give me some time to straighten things out. He grimaced and promised me that he'd hold off, but he was really pissed, so I knew that I had to do something.

Thus, it was on a dreary Saturday morning that I called a summit meeting to order, with all three of us sitting at the kitchen table.

At first we just sort of lounged around, drinking stale coffee and smoking cigarettes, the girls unresponsive to my story of the super and the bribe. I sighed a few times and finally, out of frustration, I told them both to start looking for new living space, only half bluffing.

"Oh, fuck you, Billy, you're being a real prick. I don't care what that fuckin' spick says. We're no worse than a lotta the other tenants," Pamm declared.

"Yeah, Billy. What the fuck do they want from us anyway? At least we don't bring roaches into the building. Tell 'im to leave us the fuck alone," Dexi seconded.

"Listen, I'm not losing my rent stabilized apartment because of you two assholes. It's very simple—just cut out all the yelling and screaming, otherwise I'm throwing you both out."

"Fuck you, Billy. I was here first and I'm not leaving. Who the fuck are you kidding anyway? We have sex all the time and we're like a married couple. Do you think I'm fuckin' stupid? I know how it works. After thirty days ya can't just throw somebody out. Ask the cops."

"Okay Pamm—you have a point. So how's this—do us both a favor and throw Dexi out—you brought her here. She's your friend, lover, girlfriend, whatever— you got us into this, now you get us out."

"Fuck you both. I can kick Pamm's ass anytime and she knows it. Nobody's throwing me out," stated a defiant Dexi.

"FUCK YOU DEXI—YOU SKINNY UGLY BITCH—I'LL PUNCH YOUR SKAGGY FACE IN RIGHT NOW, I'LL TAKE YOU BY THE NECK AND CHOKE THE LIVIN' SHIT OUTTA YOU, I'LL—"

"STOP SCREAMING, PAMM!! THE SCREAMING AND YELLING IS WHAT GOT US INTO THIS MESS! AND NOW YA GOT ME SCREAMIN'!"

"Oh c'mon, Billy. We can't be perfect," cried Pamm.

"Yeah, Billy," whined Dexi, mocking her.

"Look, I've had it with all this shit. If I get any more threats from the super I'll do whatever it takes. I'm just a poor guy tryin' to survive and I'm not about to lose this place."

With that I walked out of the room, went to the bathroom and took a shower. A little bit later I left the apartment and went to the supermarket. It was a Saturday, a day off from work and this is what it was like. In a word, it sucked.

21

It was Christmas rush at the clinic, the busy season, and almost every day as soon as I punched in there was an admission waiting for me. All of these extra admissions meant that I had less time for my other duties, so now I was falling behind on my paperwork and had little time to stop my patients for mandatory counseling.

The winter was rough on the clinic staff as well as the patients, and every night after work the thoughts in my head ran amuck.

That one armed guy is crying because he's been waiting for three hours to get admitted and he's hurting. He needs his methadone. NOW!! Go up to the front desk to do a supervised urine but be careful when you give the guy the bottle because he ain't got no fingers. No fingers? No fingers—not even stubs. YIKES!! Can barely keep from throwing up because so many of these patients are sickly and disgusting, like the admission I did for that Italian punk from Bensonhurst—his fuckin' face is full of Karposi sarcoma lesions and why can't he go to some fuckin' clinic in Brooklyn—YECCH!! Nobody in this hell on earth is normal and it's a never-ending horror show.

On and on it goes, from the homeless couple with the croupy infant who need to get on the program so that they can qualify for SSI and an apartment in a city housing project and get out of the shelter to the old man who comes back to the clinic right after he's been medicated because he just got mugged and he needs carfare to get home. He needs to see the doctor because they busted his nose and he's bleeding all over the place but all he wants is a subway token…these lunatics are a real trip.

Then, by the middle of January it seems to slow down a little which only means that I don't have as many freaks to tend to; oh there's still plenty of new customers, just not as many.

By now I'm just going through the motions, which is good because it means that I'm becoming desensitized, like one day when I had to do an intake on this 18-year-old girl from Long Island. I didn't even flinch when she stuck out her arms for inspection and I saw that they were all scarred up. Horrible jagged scars. Somebody new might have winced, I just noted it in her psycho-social history. Let medical ask her if she's a self-mutilator.

Oh brother, I think, when I have to admit this morbidly obese middle-aged Russian-Jewish lady from Brighton Beach who is absolutely nauseating. She's about 5' 2", 300 lbs. and reeks of stale sweat, fish, and cheap booze. Her fat face is dot' these little red sores, the trademark of itch junkies everywhere. Can't wait to see her arms. Well, at least I don't have to supervise her intake urine, and how I pity the poor female counselor who does.

Oddly, that harpy Selma stays out of my way during this busy period, seemingly content to leave me alone since I come to work everyday, unlike some of the other counselors. Christ, how I hate this fuckin' job.

22

Pamm and Dexi keep fighting and the super warns me again and Pamm won't listen to me when I tell her that Dexi's gotta go and I would throw them both out but Pamm's right, I checked it out with this lawyer I know and I can't throw Pamm out but I could throw Dexi out but if I do that Pamm will go crazy and she'll scream and yell and we'll get evicted anyway so fuck it, I'll simply suffer my destiny.

If I had any balls I'd do something but I'm burntout and depressed and I'm even losing weight and I'm tired of arguing with everybody so fuck it, I'm fucked. I'll lose my apartment, I'll lose my job, I'll lose my mind. Who cares? It's my own fault anyway for getting involved with Pamm but one night I come home from work and Pamm tells me that Dexi has moved out.

"I don't believe it."

"It's true Billy—her ratty black leather jacket is gone and so is the rest of her garbage."

I walked around the apartment and after a cursory inspection I didn't see any of her things, so I was beginning to think that it was true.

"Wow. So what happened Pamm? You're tellin' me that she left, just like that."

"Whadda you care, Billy. You wanted her out and she's out."

"Great, but would ya mind tellin' me what happened?"

"All that happened was that I put 'er down real bad. So bad that I made her cry."

"Good, good. I knew all along that all you teenaged cunts are evil. Well, ya did us both a favor. Now maybe the super will let us stay. I'll tellya this—I'm not letting her back in—no matter what."

"Chill out dude. I don't want her back."

"Good. Now maybe I won't have a nervous breakdown."

"What are you talking about?"

"Forget it."

"Oh, Billy, by the way, you're looking pretty good these days. You've lost a lotta weight. I like you like this."

"That's nice. Ever since all this shit with you and Dexi started I've been sick to my stomach—ya know, from aggravation, so I haven't been able to eat much. If it wasn't for you, I'd still be fat. Thanks, Pamm."

"Shuddup, Billy. Let's go out to eat."

"I don't have much cash."

"For once I'll pay. You can bitch to me over dinner."

"I guess this is your way of apologizing for all the trouble you've caused me over Dexi and all. Right?"

"Huh?"

"Nevermind."

We went out to dinner that night and had a nice time, but something told me that we hadn't seen the last of Dexi. Sigh.

23

Female trouble continued to dog me, this time at work in the person of Lizette Soto, who was a problem from the minute she met me. The problem was that she liked me. Really liked me. She was a scrawny little thing, aged 22, and she didn't have much going for her.

But, she did have two kids—a boy, 6 and a girl, 4, and they lived in Red Hook, Brooklyn, one of the shittiest neighborhoods in New York City.

Naturally, she was on welfare and AFDC, as the fathers of her kids had long since disappeared. She didn't even know if they were dead or alive. Even worse, she wasn't much to look at. She had thin lips, stiff coarse hair that stood up, and rough, beat up looking hands. Her Taino Indian, Afro, and Caucasian genes didn't mix well and she was strange looking—an orange Puerto Rican.

She had been assigned to my caseload at random and would come to see me almost every day. At first, I tried to slough off these weird vibes I was getting by telling myself that she was just trying to work the program.

In the beginning, when she came in for dosage increases this was easy, but then when she kept coming in just to talk to me, I knew that I had a problem.

What could I do? I couldn't tell her not to see me so much, especially since she knew enough to make appointments. She wasn't a bad kid, either, and the last thing that I wanted to do was to hurt her feelings, but boy, she was one royal pain in the ass. Sometimes she would just sit there and look at me.

"Okay Lizette, what's on your mind?"

"Nut-ting. I just thought I'd come in before I got medicated."

"Well, what about the GED program that we talked about the last time?"

"Oh, I can't do all that now—with the kids and all."

"Yeah, I guess I can understand that, but if you earn a high school equivalency diploma you'll feel good about yourself. You'll be setting a fine example for your kids and you'll be in a better position to get a job."

"I guess."

"Is there anything else today?"

"No. I guess I'll go now—'bye Billy."

"Have a nice day Lizette."

I never had much trouble when it came to easing her out, but she made me feel very awkward. Occasionally she even brought in the kids, which made it even worse because then I felt obligated to be extra nice.

I supposed that to this barrio chick I was a good guy to know. To Lizette I must have seemed very respectable—he's white, he's got an education, and he's got a steady white collar job. Maybe she even told her girlfriends about me.

Then, it all piqued one afternoon when I was on my way to lunch. While I was walking along Roosevelt Avenue, trying to decide where to eat, Lizette suddenly pops up. She's right in my face and for a moment I'm stunned. As I'm standing there she grabs my arm and starts talking to me.

"Billy, yoo know I like yoo—a lotta da girls at da clinic like yoo. Take me ta lunch widt yoo. Okay?"

"Aww, c'mon honey I don't wanna be mean to you, but I can't. It's against clinic policy. In fact I could get in big trouble just for talking to you out here. I could get fired and you could get in trouble for loitering—you know the rules. I'm sorry Lizette but I gotta go."

As I began to walk away she started stammering some nonsense about one of her junky girlfriends. She was trying to tell me that her friend was on some other program and that the girl was dating her counselor and it was great and this and that and the other thing and that she would never drop the dime on me if we got it on. All I could do was leave her standing there in mid-sentence, quite the pathetic creature.

A few days later I was the pathetic creature as I was called on the carpet by Selma over this. Apparently someone did drop the dime on me, and perhaps that someone was Lizette.

Selma looked very smug as she sat there staring at me, and as she started to speak I nervously shifted around in my chair, not knowing what to think.

"Billy, we have a serious matter to discuss. Someone from the clinic said they saw you fraternizing with one of the female patients on your caseload, this girl named Lizette Soto. Is this true?"

"Yes and no. Yes I was talking to her, no I wasn't fraternizing with her."

"Call it whatever you want to Billy. The point is that appearances are very important and the fact that you were seen hanging out with her in broad daylight is very bad."

"Aww, c'mon Selma—don't make it sound worse than it was. For the record, I have absolutely no personal interest in Lizette Soto. The whole thing started with her frequent visits to my office. Apparently she has some sort of crush on me and she won't leave me alone. A typical case of transference, I suppose."

"Well then, why didn't you come to me before it got out of hand."

"It hasn't gotten out of hand. She ambushed me on the street during my lunch break, talking all sorts of nonsense about how she and I could get together, and I gently explained that it was against clinic policy and that I wasn't buying."

"Still, Billy, you messed up. If anything like this happens again it could mean your job."

"I understand that. The next time a patient approaches me on the street I'll run away."

"Don't get smart."

"I'm not—I'm just saying that this is what I'm gonna do if any of 'em tries to talk to me on the street."

"That's enough Billy. You can go back to whatever you were doing."

"Thank you."

"Oh—and I'm taking her off of your caseload."

"Good idea."

Great idea. Why not take ten more off while you're at it. I already have more than my fair share of patients and you need me more than I need you because I'm one of the best counselors in this whole fuckin' place— that's what I wish I could have told her—that, and fuck you. Maybe someday.

24

One lonely Sunday afternoon while Pamm was messing around with a few bags I smoked a joint and gazed out of my bedroom window, watching the scene along B and 7th. As several homeless guys straggled along with no place to go and no reason to live, I finished the joint and got up to get a beer.

When I got back to the window I immediately noticed this old shopping bag lady. The poor thing was trying to cross the street and she must have been at least seventy.

Even worse, she was clad in nothing more than a thin housecoat and was on crutches. Her right leg was all red and swollen and was covered with scabs and skin ulcers. It looked like a rotten bratwurst sausage and I wondered if it was gangrenous. The foot of the bratwurst leg went uncovered, but the left one was encased in a dirty old white sneaker, sans sock.

I laughed so hard that I almost pissed in my pants as I watched her attempts to navigate the street. Every time the walk sign flashed she'd make it about a quarter of the way through and then be forced to hobble back as the light turned green. Impatient drivers honked furiously and cabbies yelled obscenities at her each time she got caught in the middle of traffic.

This pathetic spectacle came to a climax when she fell, stopping all vehicles. Suddenly it wasn't so funny, and I would have rushed out to help her, only I was too stoned.

Mercifully, a couple of street smart Puerto Rican girls from the nabe picked her up and guided her across, yelling their "fuck yous" at the screaming and honking motorists who wouldn't give the old wretch a break. For New York, it was a beatific moment.

25

Monday I'm off to work and when I approached the subway stairs at the 8th Street station I noticed this black bum standing ominously at the mouth of the entrance, holding two paper coffee cups.

I instinctively avoided him as I shot down the staircase, and when I was about halfway down the stairs I heard this horrifying shriek. I quickly turned around to see the fucking subhuman piece of shit scurry away, and this well-dressed young woman collapse in tears.

Then, while I was trying to figure out what the hell was going on, my nostrils were assaulted by this funny smell—OH NO!! THE FUCKIN' BUM HAD DRENCHED HER WITH A CUP OF PISS!

I gotta get outta this insane asylum of a town, I think, as I run down to the subway platform. Yesterday the bag lady and today the bum with piss. Degenerates who toss piss on you if you don't give them money. How much worse could it get?

Much worse. Later that day when I'm on my lunch break I just happen to spot this big fat white welfare bitch from the clinic dragging her five-year-old son by the arm, yelling and screaming at him over who knows what. The bitch was pulling on the little boy's arm so hard that I was afraid that she'd pull it off.

Enraged, I ran up to them, blocking their way. Stunned, she lets go of him.

"Oh, I recognize you. You work at the clinic. Right?"

"Right. And I swear, if I ever see you roughing up this kid again I'm gonna call the cops and have you busted and have your son taken away from you."

"Ah-ah-I'm sorry—I was having a bad day. I shoulda nevah been so mean to Robby. Please don't get me in trubble. I'm really a very good mutha."

"I'll bet. I'm gonna have a little talk with the clinic administration about what I saw here today. You better learn how to control yourself."

"I will. I promise."

I bent down to hug Robby and I told him what a wonderful little boy he was. Blond, blue-eyed, and cherubic, I managed to get a wan smile out of him. With so many childless couples looking to adopt, fate assigns him to this bottom feeder. What a pity.

The very next day, another issue involving a patient's child comes to my attention, only this kid ain't so cute. He's the son of this jack-off on my caseload named Ed Hegarty who's ticked off because "this sonofabitch judge" recently sentenced his boy to prison.

Some boy—19 years old, and all junior did was pummel this Pakistani pizza deliveryman's face to a pulp, "accidentally" breaking his nose before taking the poor schmoe's cash. He didn't mean it and it was only his second brush with the law (i.e., the second time he got caught).

Hegarty needed a sounding board, so I did my job and held my tongue as he went on and on. I couldn't take it anymore, though, when he burst out laughing as he told me how his asshole offspring was eating stolen pizza when the cops nabbed him.

It was at that point that I mumbled something about having to see another patient, and as I hustled him out of my office he was still laughing.

These lunatics were really getting on my nerves and they made me think more about my own lunatic, Pamm. While there was very little that I could do for the patients at the clinic, maybe I could do more to help her. After all, she was all I had.

Compared to a lot of the others Pamm wasn't really all that fucked up, and I felt that I had to do something, so on the train ride home that night I decided to give it a try. My efforts would begin as soon as I got home. Perhaps there was hope for this throwaway street trollop yet.

26

I knocked on the apartment door, and as soon as Pamm opened it I handed her this big brown paper bag.

"What's this?"

"Dinner. I picked us up some pastrami sandwiches and knishes and stuff from the Second Avenue Deli."

"Jew food?"

"Yeah. And it wasn't cheap and it's kosher so you better like it."

"Maybe I will. I'm sick of Chinese and pizza anyway."

"Good. Do me a favor and get dinner ready while I get washed up."

"Okay."

I took a leak and showered, and by the time that I got back to the kitchen everything was laid out nicely. I took this as a good omen.

"Hey Billy, this ain't bad. The sandwiches are rad and these potato pie things are great. Even the mustard's cool."

"Yeah. That's why I got it. I figured that it was time for something different. By the way, those potato pies are called knishes."

"Ka-what?"

"Knishes. KA-NISH-IS."

"Whatever."

"Ya know, Pamm, I'm curious—what are you?"

"What are you?"

"Oh c'mon. I don't mean it nasty. I just mean what's your ancestry?"

"What are you talking about?"

"Ancestry, ya know, like I'm Irish, the food's Jewish. What are you?"

"I'm French and Polish. What difference does it make?"

"I dunno. I'm interested in you, so I wanted to know."

"You're weird Billy."

"So I'm weird. Look, I wanna tell you a story."

"A story?"

"Yeah. Something happened at work today and it got me thinking. What happened was that this asshole patient came to my office and he tells me his wild story about how his worthless scumbag son got busted. The creep beat the shit outta this pizza delivery guy and steals his money and some pizzas and this patient has the balls to say that the judge is a son of a bitch for sending the kid to jail."

"Yeah, that's a good one. I've heard a lotta stories like that—especially since I've moved to New York."

"I'm not finished yet—the point is that this fuckin' idiot patient is mad at the judge and not his kid—that's why I'm tellin' you this."

"So?"

"So, what I'm tryin' to say is that so many of the patients are lost causes but you're not, Pamm."

"Thanks. That's good to know. Now shut up. You're getting on my nerves."

"I'm sorry. I don't blame you for getting annoyed with me. All I'm saying is that a guy like this is so whacked out that he doesn't even know that it's wrong for his son to commit this violent crime, and then he comes to my office blaming the judge and he's not even the least bit concerned about the poor pizza guy. I can't help a person like this, but I can help you, Pamm."

"You are helping me Billy. You're letting me stay here and we get along okay."

"I know all that but I wanna do more. You gotta start taking life more seriously. You gotta get your act together."

"LEAVE ME THE FUCK ALONE!"

"Calm down. I just want what's best for you. All you do is live with me and get stoned. You can at least try to work the methadone program better. Tell 'em to up your dosage."

"Fuck you, Billy."

"Fuck you, too. Look, how about this — see a qualified therapist who specializes in addiction issues—somebody who can get into your head. I'll be happy to pay for it."

"I'm not going to a shrink, so just shut up."

"Okay, Pamm. I can't make you go. But, if you change your mind just let me know and——"

"I'M NOT GONNA DO IT—SO JUST SHUT UP ABOUT IT!!"

"Okay, Pamm. Okay."

Sigh.

27

On the job for less than a year, one day Jan summons me into her office to tell me that I am now a "senior counselor."

What this means is that I get to help Selma train the new hires, a prospect that leaves me feeling less than thrilled.

My misgivings are justified when a few days later this new guy named Brad comes to see me. He's a short stocky nerd with a pierced eyebrow and a buzz cut and he's upset about something.

What's wrong Brad? I'm gay. So what? Well, Billy, when I was hired I didn't know that I'd have to do supervised urines and I feel funny about it. Why? It's just a part of the job. Yeah, but I don't think that anyone is gonna like the idea of a gay guy looking at the patients' cocks. Listen, Brad, nobody's tellin' ya to stare at their cocks—just make sure that they piss in the bottle and don't worry about it. I don't see what the problem is. Yeah, I guess you wouldn't, Billy. No Brad, I guess I wouldn't. If you wanna make an issue outta this take it up with Jan or Selma. Look, maybe I can teach you about dosage levels and intake interviews— ya know, stuff that's more directly related to your job. I don't think so, Billy. Thanks. SLAMM!!

Wow. At least once or twice a week someone new comes to my office and most of 'em are flakes. Knock, knock. Come in. Hi, I'm Stephanie. Hi Stephanie. Hi Billy—listen Billy, I'm not sure if I can work here. But you just started Stephanie. The patients on your caseload really need a counselor. What's the problem? The problem is that I don't believe in punitive actions against patients and that's all this place is about.

I dunno Stephanie, maybe you have a point but I wouldn't say that that's *ALL* this place is about. Ya know, the patients are supposed to try and work the program. What are you talking about Billy? Do you think that it's right that we make the patients follow all of these arcane rules and then we penalize them because of their illness? Look Stephanie, I don't wanna get into any debates about treatment modalities but you should understand that being on a methadone program is a privilege, not a right, and that most of 'em don't give a shit about anything but doin' drugs. Most of these characters aren't into getting off heroin—they're here because they don't wanna get sick when they can't score. If we didn't have rules then this place would be even worse. Don't patronize me, Billy. I don't agree with you and I only came in here because Jan told me to see you if I needed help with anything. Yeah, that's true. Tomorrow you can watch me do an adm
I'll even help you get caught up with your ch

want. How's that? No, that's quite all right. Thank you for your time.

Wow! What was that? This stupid prissy little twit who doesn't know her ass from her elbow is talking to me like I don't know what *I'M* doing? You better not come back here you callow naif 'cause next time I'm not gonna be so polite. Wait 'til the patients get a hold of you—I'll bet that you don't last a month, you silly bitch.

Then, as if these fools weren't bad enough, one day after work I bump into Dexi. OH! Dexi! How are you? Not so good Billy.

Hey Billy, can I move back in with you? I'm sick of that stinkin' squat. Uh—sorry Dexi—no. Oh c'mon. Just for a little while? I'm tired of panhandling and I feel so dirty all the time. Please? No, I'm sorry. Whyyyy?…Because it didn't work out with you and Pamm and I don't want no trouble with the super. FUCK YOU BILLY!! ONE DAY I'M GONNA CUT YOUR BALLS OFF AND MAKE PAMM EAT 'EM!! YOU MUTHAFUCKA!! DID PAMM TELL YOU WHAT SHE SAID TO ME? I SWEAR—ONE DAY I'M GONNA GET BOTH A YOU MUTHAFUCKAHS!! AHM GONNA CUT YOU BOTH UP REAL BAD AND YORE GONNA BE SORRY THAT YOU…

I ignored her and walked away, leaving her ranting and raving on Avenue A as curious onlookers watched as she continued to freak out.

During dinner that night I tell Pamm about this unexpected treat and she nods.

"What? Ya mean she's pulled the same sorta shit on you?"

"Yeah. The other day when I went out for cigarettes she starts following me and yellin' at me. She says she's gonna do this to me, do that to me, blah, blah, blah…"

"How'd ya get rid a her?"

"I didn't. She followed me all the way back here but she didn't have the nerve to follow me into the building. If she did I would have kicked her ass."

"I dunno Pamm. She's crazy. I don't think you could."

"I know I could. Look, I don't wanna talk about that loser anymore. Lemme know if she hassles you again. I know people who can take care of her."

"Yeah, right."

"I don't care if you don't believe me."

"I believe you, I believe you. The whole thing with her is just so weird."

"I know."

Ooh. What a quirky life I led. Crazy job, crazy neighborhood, crazy city. Christ. What a stupid fuckin' ridiculous life.

28

Time passes. I had somehow survived my baptism of fire at work and my ups and downs with Pamm, and all that I really wanted to do was to hold on to what little I had. I was very interested in keeping my problems to a minimum and staying out of trouble.

Unfortunately, sometimes trouble finds you. Like on the day when I was eating lunch near the clinic, and this patient named Richard Katowicz approaches me. Oh, great. Just what I need. Now what does this fat schmuck want?

"Billy, I just came in here to buy the paper. Honest. I'm going home right now. Please don't report me."

"Report you? For what?…Oh, yeah, that's right. Loitering. Thanks, Katowicz. You know the rules. You're supposed to get outta the neighborhood as soon as you're finished with the clinic. If someone sees me talking to you they might get the wrong idea and then it's both our asses. Now I *gotta* report you."

"Oh please, Billy. Selma said that if I got caught loitering again I was gonna get kicked outta the program. Please, Billy, please. I swear, I'll never loiter again."

"Yeah, great. Just get the fuck outta here, you fat asshole. I won't tell on you because I'm not a fink, but if I get in trouble over this I'm gonna be really pissed. Just get the fuck outta here."

Poor Katowicz. For a few seconds he just stood there quivering, a quarter ton of fun, then he just slinks away. I felt bad about insulting him but he deserved it. He knew the rules. They all did.

Loitering—another motherfucking cross that we all had to bear. By rights I should have reported him. The clinic policy against it was a necessary evil, and it was a fact that all methadone clinics had anti-loitering policies.

So, by clinic standards if a patient waited for a bus near a diner this was not loitering. However, if a patient went into that same diner for a few seconds to buy the afternoon paper, that *WAS* loitering. Therefore, the rule against loitering meant that each and every patient had better scram after finishing up at the clinic—or else.

The anti-loitering policy was enforced by loitering patrols, whereby counselors would pair off at assigned locations at various times looking for violators. Thus, if a patient was caught hanging out at some local store or coffee shop he would be reported.

Anti-loitering policies were intended to prevent frictions between patients and members of the local community, and towards this end they were effective. From time to time we'd get a c
someone about our patients, but in gen
administration did a pretty good job in th

Not that they had much choice. If things got out of hand on account of patients hassling merchants or making deals or anything else, Dailey would lose his cash cow and that would be that. Community opposition would make it impossible for the clinic to operate in the community, and as such we had to be good guests.

I had no problem with the anti-loitering policy, even if I did throw Katowicz a break. If I caught him again I'd be sure to report him, and if they threw him out, good. Just one less loser to worry about.

29

Katowicz was one thing, but you really had to feel sorry for some of these bozos. Like one day when this middle-aged, middle class Italian-American lady on my caseload comes to me in tears.

What's wrong, Sally? OHH! BILL—EE! YOU WON'T BELIEVE IT! I won't believe what? I'LL TELLYA WHAT—ME AND RALPHIE HAD A FIGHT LAST NIGHT AND YOU'LL NEVER GUESS WHAT HE DID! Try me, Sally.

I offer her a cigarette and she calms down. Then, she tells me how her boyfriend had made enlarged photocopies of her clinic ID card and put them up all over the lobby of their tony building in Forest Hills, Queens. What could I do for her? I just sat there and doled out the cigarettes, looking sympathetic while she cried and cried. She was inconsolable.

Next, there was the big shaggy haired Jewish Vietnam vet, now a hippie, who visits me talking suicide. It's a cold, cloudy morning and I'm not prepared for this.

The doctor was in that day, so that's where I take him.

The doctor talks to him for a few minutes, calls an ambulance, and they take him to Elmhurst. Later that day I discover that they wouldn't admit him. Why, doctor? Oh, because they didn't feel that he was truly suicidal. They called me and told me that with bed space at a premium if they admitted everyone who contemplated suicide they would have to admit the whole city. Oh. But what about a VA hospital, doctor? I don't know Billy, he shrugs.

A very detached attitude. Yeah, fuck everybody. Some prick embarrasses this poor lady so bad that she can't show her face in her own neighborhood and nobody wants to help a suicidal war veteran. Who cares?

Who cares? Billy cares—at least once in a while. Like when this homie on my caseload, Juan Nieves comes to see me, death certificate in hand, begging me for emergency take home bottles so that he could attend his mother's funeral in Puerto Rico.

Juan was one of those guys that I hardly ever saw. He was a hardcore heroin addict and would be one for the rest of his life. About once a month or so I'd place a stop on him, we'd talk and he'd pay lip service to the idea of taking his treatment more seriously. It was a game.

After offering my condolences I explained that only Selma, Jan, or Dailey could authorize emergency take home bottles. I told him flat out that because of his dismal tox history his chances were slim, death certificate or no death certificate.

He shrugged when I told him that since Dailey and Jan were out of the office, Selma was his only hope. I called her on the interoffice phone, and after I told her the story she told me to bring him to her office and wait. I took this as a good sign.

We sat on the shitty old sofa by her office and waited. And waited and waited and waited. I was afraid that if I called her again I'd fuck it up for him, but Juan was getting nervous and he started begging me to do something.

"Billy, man, what's taking her so long? I wanna make a flight tonight. Please, man—knock on the door."

"Juan, let's wait just a few more minutes—she might be busy with another patient."

"Oh c'mon man, we've been waiting for over an hour. Tell 'er that I'll bring in the fuckin' body if she'll gimme the bottles."

I took a deep breath and sighed out loud. Then, I got up and knocked on the door—three light taps. A split second later Selma opened it, her face contorted in rage.

"YOU GOTTA HELLUVA LOTTA NERVE BANGING ON MY DOOR! I TOLD YOU TO WAIT!"

Mortified, I snapped, lashing back at her.

"DON'T YOU YELL AT ME! WE'VE BEEN SITTIN' ON THAT RATTY COUCH FOR A LONG TIME. WHY THE HELL ARE YOU MAKING US WAIT? YA DON'T EVEN HAVE ANYONE IN YOUR OFFICE!"

Apparently, I scared her. She ran back into her lair and slammed the door shut, but she wasn't getting off that easy. I knocked on the door again but she ignored me, so I began shouting through it.

"LISTEN, YOU—JUAN'S STILL WAITING! HE WANTS TAKE HOME BOTTLES BECAUSE HIS MOTHER JUST DIED AND HE HAS TO GO TO PUERTO RICO! WE'LL WAIT HERE ALL DAY IF WE HAVE TO!"

A few moments later she emerged. She popped open the door a crack, motioned to Juan, and he went in. Not surprisingly, she turned him down.

"Was she really bitchy about it?" I asked.

"Naa-ah. She just gave me all this bullshit about trips bottles, ya know about havin' me go to some clinic in PR, fifty miles away from where I'm gonna be. She's fulla shit. Ya know, B, you shook that bitch up good. She was white as a ghost."

"Good. I'm sick of taking her shit."

"Yeah. I just hope I didn't get choo in trubble."

"Don't worry about it. Anyway, what are you gonna do, Juan?"

"About what?"

"About the funeral—the bottles. Whadda ya think I mean?"

"Oh, I guess I'll havta cop in da city tonight and bring the dope widt me. I'll cop about twenty bags."

"Are you fuckin' crazy?"

"What else can I do? I'll tuck the bags up my ass and use it all up in PR. I'll cop some more on my way home from the airport."

"You're nuts. Don't forget, you'll have to be reinstated back in to the clinic if you miss more than two days in a row. But I'll tell you what, see me when you get back. I'll personally reinstate you."

"Thanks, man. Yeah, ya know I seen you around the lower east side. You live around there?"

"Not far. I live in the East Village."

"Figures. Thanks, Billy."

30

Pamm was unhappy and I didn't know how to help her. She slept a lot and she wasn't eating and, worst of all, she wasn't paying much attention to her personal hygiene. In fact, her pussy stank. So, over dinner one night I confronted her.

"Pamm, what's wrong? You've been very down and you've been like this for days. Please tell me why you're so blue."

"I'm okay, Billy. I'm just a little depressed."

"That I can tell, but why?"

"You're a fool, Billy. I'm a junky whore on methadone, living with some fucking guy who can throw me out at any time, and you ask me 'What's wrong?' Are you fuckin' stupid?"

"You're right, you're right, but what else is wrong?"

"All right, I'll tell ya. I called my mom last week and she told me to fuck off. I only called her because I felt so alone—no other reason. We hadn't spoken in

120

over a year and that's how she acts. My own fuckin' mother doesn't give a shit if I live or die. How's that?"

I looked down at the table and then back at her. What could anyone say in a situation like this?

"Uh, Pamm. Thank you for tellin' me, ya know, for taking me into your confidence. Listen, my family story ain't too great either. As far as I'm concerned, blood means nothing."

"Oh, shut up."

"Oh, c'mon Pamm. I'm just tryin' to help. And look, I'd never throw you out. You know that."

"That's what you say now. What about six months from now?"

"What about if the sun collides with the moon? I'd never throw you out."

"I dunno, Billy. I wish I was dead. I feel like committing suicide."

"Well, ya know something Pamm, a few weeks ago this guy on my caseload comes to me and he's also talking about suicide. You probably know 'im by sight. Anyway—me, you, him—I don't know why like half the people on the planet don't commit suicide. I don't. I read the papers, I watch the news—I really don't."

"So. What's your point?"

"There is no point — except maybe that I understand how you feel because I often feel the same way as you."

"Bullshit."

"I do, I do. Believe me, I do. I get very unhappy but it usually passes in a few days. Do you think it's easy being a big fat failure? I'll be thirty-one soon and what do I have to show for my life?"

"I'm sorry, Bill. Now I'm bummin' you out."

"Don't be sorry. At least you're talking to me about it."

"I guess. Listen Billy, talking to you has helped. Really. I never knew that you could be like this."

"Like what?"

"Shut up, Billy. I don't wanna talk anymore."

"Okay."

"Okay."

31

It was almost summer and I had grown complacent. Perhaps it was this complacency that our old foe Dexi sensed when she approached Pamm and I one night. We were waiting for a light at Avenue B and 10th Street when she stopped us.

"Hey Billy. Hey Pamm. Where ya goin'?"

Pamm and I looked at each other, looked at Dexi, and then looked straight ahead. We kept walking east, trying our best to shake her, but she wasn't having any of it. She was on our asses, yelling at us, spewing all sorts of curse words and acting like a maniac.

She kept following us and the more that we tried to ignore her, the more intent she was on making a scene. Finally, we stopped in front of this news kiosk on A and St. Mark's, both of us at our wits' end.

"Dexi, what do you want?"

"Gimme five bucks and I'll leave you alone."

I reached for my wallet but Pamm stopped me.

"Don't give her no money, Billy. What the fuck is wrong with you?"

"SHUT UP PAMM!! DON'T LISTEN TO HER BILLY—GIMME FIVE BUCKS AND I'LL LEAVE YOU ALONE FOR A WHILE," Dexi shrieked.

For a while? What am I fuckin' nuts? This is extortion. Pamm's right. If I give her the dough, every time she sees me she'll hit me up for money. The platinum sewer rat can drop dead. I'm not giving her squat.

We kept moving, pretending not to hear her as she stalked us. She's a psychopath, Pamm. Tell me about it, Billy. So what do we do? I don't know. Maybe she'll collapse or something.

We were quite the stoic pair as we glided along. Then, just as we reached the corner of A and 7th she jumped in front of us, blocking our way.

"Billy…do something," Pamm pleaded.

"Dexi, do I have to call the cops? I will if you don't fuck off."

She smiled this slow, demented smile and reached into the left front pocket of the old ratty leather jacket. I thought that she was reaching for a cigarette. It was not a cigarette.

I didn't know what it was, all I knew was that it was some sort of small solid object and that she was trying to hit me with it. It all happened so fast, but I recall that I instinctively raised my right hand to block it. The moment that I did I felt a sharp pain, followed by a heavy trickle of blood. Now it was obvious what she had done. THE CRAZY BITCH STABBED ME!!

Right after it happened my first impulse was to run back to my apartment to assess the damage, but fortunately I wasn't calling the shots. The next thing

I know is that Pamm's screaming, passersby are hovering, and someone's running out of a restaurant with a damp towel.

While Pamm's busy crying and this good Samaritan is wrapping the towel around my injured hand somebody must have dialed 911, because minutes later the cops were there with an ambulance. Meanwhile, Dexi had ran away, successfully evading anyone who may have tried to stop her.

While I was whisked away to Beth Israel Hospital, I marveled at all of the attention that I was getting. Wow. I felt like a celebrity and everyone was so nice, even the cops.

Pamm was in the ambulance with me, and in less than ten minutes I was being attended to by a nurse and a doctor. A fat, florid Italian-American cop stood by, waiting for the doctor to finish up so that he could take my statement.

Quite honestly, I was too dazed to be frightened. My hand seemed to be working okay, so I assumed that the wound was superficial and I guessed right.

First, the young Filipino nurse poured some sort of bluish-green antiseptic into it and then the middle-aged, bespectacled Jewish doctor treated me. His name was Resnoff.

"Mister Selkirk, you're very lucky. What we have here is a shallow vertical knife wound, roughly four centimeters long. The assailant caught you right near the edge of the palm. Had the knife penetrated just a bit more there would have been nerve damage and you would have lost some normal functioning. You don't need stitches, but I'm sending you home with a bottle of amoxicillin and some simple instructions. I want to see you the day after tomorrow so that I can make sure that the wound is healing properly. Any questions?"

"Uh—I guess not, but thank you doctor."

"The nurse will give you a tetanus shot and after that the police want to talk to you."

The nurse gave me the injection and handed me the bottle of amoxicillin, along with written instructions. When she was done, the officer helped me out of the chair and into this small room near the reception desk.

"Sorry about your injury, guy. This'll only take a few minutes. Ya want some coffee?"

"I guess so."

"Good. I'll be right back."

Five minutes later he was back with the coffee. He sat down at the small table and took out his big fat leather notebook, the kind that all NYPD cops have. I wondered how the cops could run with those things stuffed into their back pockets.

First, he asked me if there were any witnesses and then he insisted on fixing my coffee.

"Uh, yeah, officer. My girlfriend Pamm was with me. She saw the whole thing. I think she's waiting for me."

"Is she that skinny blonde girl who was standing right near you in the street, crying?"

"Yeah. Where is she?"

"I saw her in the waiting room by the nurses' station before. Wait here, I'll see if she's still there."

A short time later he was back with Pamm. It was almost midnight and she looked terrible, but who cared? I was just happy to see her.

Pamm sat down with us, and no sooner than she did the cop starts giving us the third degree. It was like, Who stabbed you? Why did she stab you? What were you two doin' down there? WHAT? WHAT? WHAT?

Pamm and I looked at each other as if to say, "What is this fucker talking about?"

We told him exactly what happened, explaining our relationship to Dexi, as he sat there impassively taking notes.

When he was done with us he flipped the black leather flap over his pad and gave us the number of the local precinct. It was obvious that he felt that we were a couple of lowlifes, but what did we care? We didn't like him either. Let the fat red-faced fascist pig go back to his fat ugly wife in Ronkonkoma or wherever the fuck he lived and let 'im file his fuckin' report.

Pamm hailed a cab and by 1 a.m. we were back home. My hand throbbed some, but mostly I was exhausted and so was Pamm.

That fuckin' Dexi—if I ever get a hold of her she's dead meat. That fuckin' sewer rat got me good tonight and the cops don't give a shit and on top of that I bet I owe the hospital a lotta money, insurance or no insurance.

Die Dexi, you evil bitch.

32

The next morning over coffee Pamm couldn't do enough for me. She made us breakfast and she kept saying how sorry she was for getting us mixed up with Dexi. I kept telling her that it wasn't her fault, but it did no good and she couldn't stop blaming herself.

At 10 a.m. sharp I called the clinic. After five rings Colleen picks up and when I told her that I wasn't coming in and why, she transfers my call to Selma.

Selma tells me that she's on another call and she puts me on hold. I wait for a full five minutes and then I hang up. Fuck her...Who the hell does she think I am, some asshole patient who's gonna wait all day for Queen Shit?

Forty minutes later the phone rings. I pick it up on the fourth ring.

"Hello?"

"Billy?"

"Selma from the clinic. I hear that you're taking the day off. Why?"

"Because I was attacked last night. I got stabbed."

"Really?"

"Yes, really. This crazy panhandler tried to shake me down and when I tried to walk away she stabbed me in the hand."

"How bad is it? Is it so bad that you can't come in? We're swamped with admissions."

"Look Selma, I was rushed to the hospital last night. It was a little on the traumatic side. I have to see the doctor tomorrow and if he approves I'll be back at work the day after tomorrow. I'll be sure to bring in a doctor's note. Goodbye."

I hung up on her because I knew that I'd lose it if I didn't. Selma was a real piece of work. Not even a twinge of sympathy. Thanks, Selma.

33

When I went back to work two days later, Colleen and a couple of the others expressed their concern for me but that was about it. Okay.

As the days pass and my wounded hand continues to heal, I try to put it behind me but it's not that easy. My hand throbs, I'll have a new scar, and I'll have to be on the lookout for Dexi, which is no laughing matter.

This crazy wench may attack me again, so I've taken to carrying pepper spray. I tell myself that if she comes near me or Pamm again I'll choke the living shit outta her, but so what? She's already won because she has me psyched out. I'm suffering from post-traumatic stress, and I don't like it.

Then, as if all this isn't enough, one morning I find that there's this strange pimple on my ass, right at the bottom of my tailbone. For a few days I try to ignore it but it keeps getting bigger and bigger. I don't know what the hell it is and soon it's so big that it feels like I'm growing another butt.

Full of anxiety, I finally go to a neighborhood clinic and the doctor tells me that it's a pilonidal cyst. He says that it's common, and explains that the cyst itself is more or less a big tuft of encapsulated ingrown hair and that it's become infected.

The region surrounding the cyst is inflamed with pus, he says, which is why it's so big and tender and hot to the touch. Yep, it's tender all right, it's so goddamn tender that it hurts like hell, especially when I try to sit down.

The GP from the clinic makes a call to this proctologist friend of his and I get an appointment for that very afternoon. Don't be alarmed, he says, I just think that you should see a specialist without delay. All right, well, thanks, doctor.

I leave the neighborhood with the name and address of this ass doctor who practices in Kips Bay and I walk there, in spite of my delicate condition. When I give the nurse my name she tells me that I won't have to wait too long, and she ain't kiddin', 'cause less than ten minutes later the doctor's telling me to drop my drawers.

After a brief probing of the hot spot, the proctologist declares that surgery can't wait, and he schedules an operation for the next day. Very self-assured, he says that the cyst excision is routine and that he's performed dozens of them. He tells me to go home and take it easy for the rest of the day and to be at the hospital tomorrow, at 7 a.m. sharp.

I go straight home like he says and as soon as I get there I tell Pamm all about it. Then, I call the clinic, I get Colleen, I explain the situation and she says that she'll let Jan and Selma know. Oh, and Billy, don't forget to bring in a doctor's note.

Early the next morning while it's still dark, Pamm and I take a cab to the hospital. She's in the admitting office with me while they ask me all of these questions, and she kisses me goodbye as they take me up to my room.

I undress down to my briefs, slip on a gown, and climb into bed. A short time later, some stupid looking CNA comes by to administer an enema, and I'm not exactly thrilled. Then, right after I'm done with the toilet, this big black fucker walks in. He's here to shave my butt. Oh, man.

I've been purged, shaved, and IV'd, and now I'm good to go, so they come for me and I'm taken to the OR. Once there, I'm removed from the gurney and placed face down on the operating table. Nurses and various medical aides hover about, and one of them injects me with some type of sedative.

Next, the anesthesiologist arrives and he tells me that he's giving me a spinal, and minutes later I can no longer feel the lower half of my body.

Finally, the proctologist waltzes in, raring to go. He mumbles something to someone, and next I hear the low whine of some sort of surgical device. He's busy at work, draining the stinking pus and cutting out the cyst, along with a sizeable piece of meat. It's at this point that I fall asleep.

When I wake up I'm in the recovery room, and a sweet young nurse is telling me that the surgery went well. Shortly after this, I'm being wheeled back into my room.

As soon as I'm tucked into bed, I fall into a deep, deep sleep.

When I get up several hours later I discover that my backside is all packed up with dressing and tape, and I'm taken aback by the sheer amount of it.

Early the next morning the doctor visits me. He tries to be pleasant, and he tells me that I can be discharged as soon as someone comes in to pick me up.

The doctor cautions me to leave the dressing alone, and he schedules me for a follow-up visit the next day. He insists that I take the rest of the week off from work, and he leaves me with a prescription bottle of Darvocet for pain. I thank him and we shake hands.

I eat my hospital lunch of meat loaf with mushroom gravy, green beans, mashed potatoes, red jello and coffee. Not bad.

When I'm finished eating I call Pamm and she's there in less than an hour. She helps me get dressed and she waits in the lobby as I check out.

I sure as hell hope that my health insurance pays for all this, I think, as we make our way past the revolving doors and on to the chilly streets.

She holds on to my left arm as she hails a cab and we're home in the blink of an eye. What a babe. The poor thing's very quiet and it's as if she thinks I'm gonna die or something. The very thought of it cracks me up, as I tell her that I'm doing fine.

I am doing fine, but I'm totally wiped out, and I tell her not to worry as I fall into bed and into another deep, deep sleep.

34

Pamm took me to the doctor the next day which was good, because I never would have made it without her. I didn't realize that the surgery was going to take so much out of me, and I wasn't feeling that great.

I was still exhausted, the deep wound left by the operation was painful and itchy, and I was becoming irritable.

The doctor cleaned out the wound and changed the dressing, reassuring me that all was well. He put me on a regimen of sitz baths, and showed me how to care for and dress the wound.

He explained that it would take a full twelve weeks for the wound to completely heal, and I was to return to his office once a week until that time. Fine. At least that grotesque mass was no longer a part of me, and for that I was grateful.

I took care of myself and I was able to go back to work the following Monday. The first morning back was kind of nice. When I handed Colleen the doctor's note she hugged me and told me not to worry. She sat me down in the office and called a few of the staffers in. They all said how happy they were to see me and they even bought me breakfast. I was speechless.

Too bad it couldn't be the same way with Selma. When I bumped into her later all I got was a terse "Hello, how are you?" and that was that. Not that I cared. As long as she kept her distance I was happy.

Since I was recovering I did only what I could, and several times during this period I came in late and punched out early.

Naturally, this pissed off Selma, which was cool, even if it meant being called on the carpet.

Billy, we must talk. Oh? Yes, I know all about your surgery but I have a clinic to run and you can't make your own hours. Yeah, well, I'll do my best to be here on time and to finish each shift, but it'll be another few weeks before I'm fully recovered. That's not good enough, Billy. Selma, if ya want I'll bring in another note. In fact, you can even speak to the doctor. That's nice Billy, but no. Just be on time and stay on for your full shift—each and every day. Sure, Selma, I'll do my best… you pockmarked ugly old harpy…If you were a guy I'd do my best to punch your fuckin' ugly face in. Bitch.

After our discussion I still wasn't perfect, but I did better—or at least good enough to get her off my case. Still, I wasn't gonna push myself too much, and if she didn't like it, tough. Let some doctor cut out a big chunk of flesh outta your tailbone and let's see how you do. Bitch.

35

Being a patient on a methadone program was a game, and no one knew the game better than Harry Weisenfelder. Harry was a throwback to the William Burroughs junky era, which was what made him so special. What a character.

At age 73, the old reprobate wasn't gonna take any shit from anyone, especially from some young whippersnapper like me.

Despite being a dope fiend for most of his adult life, Harry had managed to retire from the postal service, and he lived in an apartment in the Bronx. His only family was his 98-year-old mother, who lived in a Hebrew home for the aged not far from his home.

From day one Harry let me know that it was nothing personal, but he didn't like me. He said that he never liked any of his counselors and that methadone was a racket.

According to him, heroin should have never been made illegal for personal use, and that heroin intenance was a better idea, like the way they did it in England. He claimed that the only reason that he was even on methadone, was because he was too old to cop.

Maybe he was too old to cop, but I suspected otherwise when one of his urines came back dirty. If this old prick thought that I was gonna let him get over on account of his age or anything else, he had another thing coming. I put the stops on and just as I expected, he was all in a tizzy by the time he got to my office.

"WHO THE FUCK DO YOU THINK YOU ARE—STOPPING ME LIKE THAT! I HAVE TO BE AT THE PODIATRIST IN AN HOUR—LIFT THE STOP RIGHT NOW!!"

"I'll lift the stop as soon as I'm done talking to you. Step inside."

As we sat down in my dingy rat hole the old man was defiant.

He kept his arms crossed as he glared at me through thick horn-rimmed glasses, the kind with the old-fashioned black plastic frames.

"Listen Harry, we both know why you're here. Your last urine came back opiate positive. You're on a three day a week schedule and that's a gift from the clinic because you're elderly. If you're saying that the lab made a mistake that's one thing, and if you've been taking some type of prescription medication that's another thing, but I don't think it's anything like that. Am I wrong?"

First, he looks at his feet and then he looks up. He thrusts his owlish nose out at me, his lined face red and twisted in anger.

"OH—I'M AN OLD MAN. WHY DON'T YOU LEAVE ME ALONE?"

"Look Harry, I'm not the one making a federal case outta this…I'm not the one having a shit fit. I'm just tellin' you that the next time you come up dirty I'm gonna raise your schedule and I'm gonna have the doctor see you about a dosage increase. It's not like I have much choice. I'm just a poor hack. You know that."

"Ahh, shuddup," he said, getting up and gesturing in wild, jerky motions.

He bellows on for a few minutes about a lot of disparate stuff, not making much sense. In his worn out tweed cap, faded rust colored corduroy sport jacket and old scuffed up wing tipped shoes, he was oddly compelling. Of course, he was also crazy, but that was besides the point.

"Please Harry, calm down—there's no reason to be this upset. I'm not taking any punitive action—yet. Just try to play by the rules," I stated, interrupting his harangue.

"FUCK YOU. YOU-YOU-YOU-YOU-YOU…," he stammered.

"FUCK YOU. YOU—YOU—YOU—YOU—YOU—TOO," I mimicked.

Harry was cool. Next thing you know we're both laughing. Our meeting ends with me telling him that if he gives me any more dirty urines I'm gonna raise his schedule, and him telling me that I can go fuck myself.

All in a day's work.

36

It's a gloomy Friday afternoon and I'm at the reception desk pulling desk duty because one of the deskmen got fired the other day for loaning money from one of the patients.

All counselors worked the desk from time to time and personally, I didn't care for it. But, a job's a job, meaning that when you're working the desk you have to think like a deskman and enforce the rules.

So here I was, sitting on my barstool, ever vigilant, helping to keep the peace, when this skinny little AIDS junky asks me for a favor.

"Billy, can I use the bathroom? I really gotta go."

"No sir. Sorry. You know the rule—you've already been medicated. Dailey doesn't let the patients use the toilet after they get medicated. Sorry."

"AW, C'MON BILLY! PLEASE? IF YOU DON'T LEMME GO I'M GONNA SHIT IN MY PANTS! CAN'T YOU COUNSELORS EVER GIVE A GUY A BREAK?"

David Steier

Oh boy. Damned if I do, damned if I don't. If I say no he'll shit in his pants and I'll feel funny about it— bad karma and all. If I say yes and they find out about it I'll be in trouble. What should I do? Oh, to hell with this fuckin' rule— how much trouble can I get into just for showing an AIDS case a little compassion?

"Okay, go. Try to be quick about it."

"Thanks. I knew someone around here had to have a heart."

Five minutes later he was done. P.U.! When I opened the crapper door I gagged. For real. The poor cat. How could anyone have said no? Then again, Selma wasn't just anyone.

It was exactly ten minutes to five when my phone rang. Uh oh. Something tells me this is bad. Hello? Billy—Selma. Please come to my office immediately. Okay, Selma—I'll be right there.

I was there in less than a minute and took the chair opposite her desk. She looked me in the eye and gave it to me straight.

"Billy—you're fired."

"Why?"

"I think you know why. You let a patient use the toilet after he was medicated. You know the rules."

"Yeah, but Selma, the poor guy has AIDS. He came to me crying. He begged me. He said that he was gonna shit in his pants."

"That's not the point. The point is that Dr. Dailey and Jan both agree with me that you should be fired."

Oh man. I sit there for a few tense moments, and while I do I feel these sudden sharp pains in the region of my recently ravaged butt. Oh, Jesus.

"Ya know what Selma? You can have this crummy job. And by the way, the whole staff despises you and the patients hate you. You suck Selma, you really fuckin' suck."

She sat there expressionless as I walked away, and surprisingly, no one followed me when I went back to my office to get my things. I didn't want to push my luck by making the rounds and saying my goodbyes, so I just punched out and left the clinic for good.

The last thing that I remember seeing was this overweight Puerto Rican girl holding a baby in her arms. She was coming in as I walked out. I held the door for her as she brushed past me without saying thanks.

I felt kind of numb during that last train ride home; not bad, just numb. After I got off the train, I picked up this big pizza pie from an Italian restaurant on West 8th Street and walked home.

Pamm knew that something was up as I handed her the big flat greasy cardboard box. She put the box on the table, set up some plates and glasses, and waited for me to come out of the bathroom.

As soon as I sat down I told her the whole story. She reacted the way that a lot of people do, and she went on and on about what I should do and I how I could get even. It was good to know that she was on my side but after a good five minutes of this, I told her to shut up.

"Why are you telling me to shut up Billy?—Those fuckin' scumbags fire you for nothin' and you're gonna let 'em get away with it?"

"There's nothing that I can do about it—except apply for unemployment. Whadda ya want me to do?"

"I don't know, but if it was me I'd do something. Maybe you should go to some TV station or newspaper and they'd do a story about what a joke the place is—anything to get back at them is good."

"Na-aah. To tell ya the truth I don't even give a shit. It was a shitty job and I had a good run. Fuck it."

"You're a wimp."

"Gimme a break Pamm. Don't worry, I'll get another job."

We finished our dinner and watched some television and smoked some weed and went to bed. As I drifted into sleep I found solace in the fact that my relationship with Pamm had outlasted the job.

37

After several days the full effect of my dismissal from the clinic took hold. Sometimes I felt angry and bitter and sometimes I didn't care. Strangely, I was also energized, and from this energy sprang a fleeting sense of elation, but mostly my moods would change.

I supposed that what I was experiencing was the common angst of laid off and terminated employees everywhere. Fortunately, I still had enough sense to realize that I had to get it together before I went broke.

I decided against applying for unemployment insurance because I knew that those bastards would challenge it and probably win, arguing that I was fired for "just cause." I was also reluctant to apply because I didn't want to fall into a lazy rut again. So, I had to look for a new job, but what?

I dreaded the thought of going on job interviews and I wasn't too hot on the idea of working for another clinic, so for about two weeks I did very little. I got stoned a lot, hung out with Pamm, ate too much and became increasingly sullen. It wasn't good.

I had lost that initial energy and by this time I was just another uptight asshole. I'd snap at Pamm and anyone else who rubbed me the wrong way, and I didn't even realize how nutty I was until one sunny early winter afternoon.

It all started very innocently. I had decided to go out for a stroll, but I wasn't very focused and I just sort of rambled along. Then, before I knew it, I found myself on the corner of 42nd Street and Broadway.

Now, I'm just standing there, minding my own business, when this chubby, white, middle-aged tourist lady asks me how to get to Union Square. I politely tell her where the train station is, what train to take and where to get off, but somehow this isn't good enough.

Instead of saying thanks, she gives me this snotty, superior look. She looks at me like she thinks that I don't know what I'm talking about and she walks away. WHAT A BITCH! I felt dissed, so I ran after her.

As soon as I caught up I called her a dumb stupid bitch and kept screaming at her. I yelled that she better get out of New York because she was a fuckin' asshole who didn't know shit and that she didn't belong here. I kept at it and kept at it, never at a loss for words. Something had come over me and I just wouldn't let go.

All of this was going on right in the middle of everything, but people passed us by and didn't seem to notice. No one cared. Cops strolled by and were oblivious; traffic lights changed colors; cabs and buses rumbled past. So, unimpeded, I kept following her and following her.

Finally, she started to cry. I started to laugh. Next, I was laughing so hard that I almost peed in my pants. Then, while I'm laughing hysterically she runs away, and watching her waddle down 42nd Street made it even funnier.

As soon as I got home I told Pamm about it and then we both laughed some more. It was funny.

Later on that day, though, I realized that I was turning into a wacko and that I had to get a job, any job, to stay normal. I wasn't quite ready to go back to the 9 to 5 world, so I figured that my best bet was a short term "off the books" job. I decided to take a job as a driver for a local car service.

A car service is like a taxicab company, only not as good. In New York City, the way that it works is that city licensed cab drivers can pick up street passengers as well as dispatch calls, and all of their fares are metered.

Car service drivers can only pick up dispatch calls for set fares, and although these drivers are technically known as independent contractors, in essence the system's rigged up in such a way that a driver works off the books if he wants to work off the books.

Since I was only interested in cash money this type of deal appealed to me, and if by some freak chance the IRS found out about it, I'd worry about it then.

All you had to do to get a driving job at a car service was to go down to the garage of your choice and sign up. By contrast, if I had chosen to be a legitimate New York City taxicab driver I would have had to pay around $200 for all sorts of bullshit fees, and then I would have been forced to see their doctor for the mandatory physical.

Even worse, they also make you go to taxi school for a week with all of these fucking immigrants from countries like Tajikistan and Zambia. Fuck that shit. No way. I know how to speak English, thank you, and nobody's gonna make me join some useless union. Thanks, but no thanks—I'll take my chances with a car service.

With these thoughts in mind, I went to this garage in Chelsea where they're always hiring drivers. I come armed with a copy of my driving record from the DMV and walked into the offices of West Star Limousine. The office was located directly across the street from the garage, where the owners stored their fleet of cars. It was a cowboy operation with a very spartan set up.

The business office kind of reminded me of the clinic, where there, too, they would only give you the minimum needed to survive. There was a cashier's cage at one end of the large room, a big open area at another end where the dispatchers held court, and a small reception area near the entrance.

As soon as I walked in I went up to the reception desk and told the pockmarked, angry young Puerto Rican dude that I was there to apply for a driving job. He asked me if I had my abstract from the DMV, and when I produced it he snatched it, and gave me some forms to fill out.

I walked over to this big, long table near the vending machines, pulled up a folding chair, sat down and filled out the papers.

The good thing about this place was that I didn't have to put up any deposits. They just checked my license via some computer tracking system, told me that if I signed the papers it meant that I was waiving the right to sue them if I got hurt in an accident, and that if I missed a shift I was fired.

I just shrugged, and a short time later some tough looking Chinese hip hop kid comes out and asks me if I want to work tonight. I tell him yes, and the next thing I know he gets on the walkie talkie and orders someone from the garage to pull a car up.

We leave the office and jump into this beat up old dark blue Buick Century with West Star insignias on the doors, and my tenure with this company begins. The Chinese guy sits in the driver's seat and shows me how to work the radio, warning me to pick up the mike whenever I hear my car number called by the dispatcher. Then, he asks me if I have any questions, I say no, he gives me the keys and I'm on my own. Cool.

I'm working a twelve hour shift (as is customary in this business) from 6 p.m. to 6 a.m., and it's almost six. I'm anxious and excited as I try to psyche myself up for the long night ahead, hoping to gross about one hundred bucks. I figure that after I pay for gas at West Star's private gas station (as required, at rip-off prices) and give the bastards their fifty percent, I can clear around forty dollars.

About ten minutes later I go on my first call. No big deal, just an elderly couple going to a neighborhood restaurant—a five dollar fare with a fifty cent tip. Wow. I wait a few minutes for my next call and it's another small fare, and so it goes all night.

True, sometimes it gets a little scary when I get runs uptown, to places like Harlem and Morningside Heights, but so far it doesn't seem too horrible.

In a way I even like it. I get a front row view of the city at night, I get to take several long breaks and eat in the diners, and the long hours fly right by. I make it through the first night in one piece and except for the fact that I'm dog tired, my recently operated on butt aches, and I've only cleared $37.68, it wasn't too bad.

I ride the crosstown train home and when I get in Pamm's asleep. I take a long hot shower and check out my tailbone. I had recently seen the doctor who told me that it was all closed up and healed, and I'm relieved to find that I haven't done any damage. Still, I'm mad at myself for not thinking about my butt before taking this gig. Oh well, I'll try to stick it out for a while, I think, as I slip into bed next to Pamm.

I fall into a deep, deep sleep right away, but the alarm clock goes off six hours later and it seems like six minutes. I drag myself out of bed feeling all exhausted and sluggish, but otherwise I'm okay.

I have just enough time to make myself dinner and relax awhile before heading down to the garage. Pamm's nowhere to be found. I feel like talking to her but she's out, so tough. I listen to the radio and joylessy eat my ham and eggs and drink my coffee.

My second night holds no surprises and I continue to work at this strange and shitty job five nights a week, including Saturday, naturally the busiest night.

All of this driving in stop and go traffic has turned me into a sodden lump of clay, and after about a month of this torture I'm burnt-out. On a good night I make only sixty or seventy bucks and I'm averaging about $300 a week. That's less than six bucks an hour, so it hardly seems worth it.

Nevertheless, I plod on—until one night when my career as a professional driver literally comes to a screeching halt.

The first few hours of my final night were unexceptional. There were just the usual quirks and annoyances that come with the job. I start off with this black businessman who gives me a five dollar tip on a ten dollar fare, probably because he was so flabbergasted by the fact that a native New York white guy would take him up to Harlem.

Then, I stopped for coffee and cigarettes, and next, I picked up these two little JAPS (Jewish American Princesses) who both had shit fits when I couldn't drop them off directly in front of their building, because of all of these double parked cars.

They started to raise hell but they shut up fast when I screamed at them, telling them to "Give me my money and get the fuck out." They left shaking, shocked I suppose by the fact that someone as lowly as a livery driver would dare to raise his voice to them.

The next few passengers were normal, but then I get this asshole who starts complaining to me that the car smells like piss. Maybe it did smell like piss, I didn't know. By this time my sense of smell had probably dried up; the point was that it wasn't my fault and I didn't want to hear it. He wouldn't shut up so I made him get out. He huffed and puffed a lot but he didn't have much choice because I stopped the car and wouldn't move. I didn't make him pay me, I just kicked him out.

That night I had a few calls that kept me in the Times Square area and I enjoyed these fares. What a neighborhood and what a stupid job. Get dissed, get hissed and come to 42nd Street. True, it was more fun here when the hookers and street people ruled, but I still enjoyed this part of town.

This was the job—the assholes, the cool people, the dangers, the discomfort and the annoyances. Bad brakes, however, weren't in the contract. The cars in this fleet were barely roadworthy because of the way those cowboys ran the business, so the brakes on my vehicle were shot and I had an accident.

It was a nothing accident and it didn't even involve anyone else. All that happened was that I hit this blue wooden NYPD sawhorse that the cops had placed in the middle of 28th Street, between 5th and 6th, for reasons only known to them.

It was very foggy that night and the damn thing was barely visible. I braked ten feet in front of it but the brakes crapped out and I hit it, taking out the right headlight.

I had about three hours to go on my shift, and since I couldn't drive with one headlight I drove the car back to the garage.

I told the greasy Jamaican dispatcher on duty what had happened and he immediately starts cursing me out. At first I get mad and start screaming back at him, but then I come up with this brilliant idea. Just go. I haven't cashed out yet and I've grossed over one hundred bucks tonight, so go. I take the money and run.

What can they do? The cashier and the dispatcher can't come running after me because they have to stay where they are. They both know that if they leave their stations all sorts of chaos could ensue, so I briskly walk away, leaving the Jamaican asshole sputtering. Ten minutes later I'm back in the East Village, laughing about the whole thing.

It's three in the morning and the adrenaline is flowing as a wave of exhilaration begins to set in. What a crazy town—it's like a great big carnival out here with busy restaurants, heavy traffic, and sidewalks thick with pedestrians at this time of night. Unbelievable.

I walk around the neighborhood until the exhilaration fades and exhaustion follows. I make my way slowly down the street where I live, walk up the stairs and unlock the door. Pamm's sitting in the dark, half asleep, smoking a cigarette. She mutters something as I take the cigarette away from her dangling hand and snuff it out.

A momentary compulsion seizes me and I want to wake her up and tell her about my latest misadventure, but I think better of it and let it go.

Instead, I pull up the hardback chair that's by the window and turn it towards her. The room is illuminated by the neon street lamps, and the light hits Pamm's face in such a way that it turns her into a work of art.

What an epic moment. The girl looks absolutely beatific and she's sitting in my living room. I sit there for a very long time watching her sleep, and I only get up when I feel myself dozing off.

I go to the bedroom, take off my shoes and socks and lay on top of the bed, without even bothering to change or get under the covers. I'm too tired and that would take too much effort.

I must have been asleep for about an hour when Pamm runs into the bedroom, screaming at the top of her lungs, scaring me like I've never been scared before.

"BILLY GET UP!! GET UP YOU ASSHOLE—THE BUILDING'S ON FIRE!!"

I slowly got up and I looked at her. Her face was beet red and sweaty and she keeps shrieking at me like a madwoman. She had her leather jacket on and was carrying a couple of white plastic bags, the kind you get at the supermarket.

Boy, was I glad that I was already dressed. I heard all sorts of yelling and screaming from the Puerto Ricans upstairs and all of these other wild sounds.

I put on my socks and shoes and grabbed my wallet and winter coat, not fully awake yet. I hesitated for a few seconds and Pamm starts beating me. We could both smell the smoke and feel the heat.

She was punching me in the arms and shoulders, spit flying out of her mouth, snot coming out of her nose, and I finally start to move. Seconds later we run out of the apartment and within a minute we were out of the building.

It was cold outside. Pamm was crying and shivering but I just stood there. I counted two police cars, two ambulances, and three fire trucks. Pamm and I never had much to do with the other tenants in the building, but now everyone was exchanging sympathetic glances and talking.

A couple of little Hispanic kids who lived on the fourth floor were mesmerized by everything, while the old Ukrainian lady from the first floor was taken by ambulance to a nearby hospital. From what I had overheard, the fire had started in the first floor vestibule and she was suffering from smoke inhalation.

The cops and some inspector from the Fire Department were all over me and Pamm and everyone else, asking us all of these questions that we couldn't answer. Apparently, they suspected that the fire was the work of an arsonist.

While they were questioning us the fire blazed on. Since we lived on the third floor I had some small hopes that we could salvage a few things, but right now that was neither here nor there.

The cops told us that someone had dumped a bunch of old clothes near the rear of the first floor, doused them with an accelerant, lit the pile, and split.

The fire chief gave us his card, told us that we could qualify for assistance from the city, and asked us to call him if we heard anything or had any suspects in mind.

Pamm and I looked at him, nodded, and then looked at each other. We both had an idea about the arsonist. Perhaps our white trash friend from West Virginia did it. Perhaps. Or perhaps it was the landlord trying to get rid of us rent stabilized leeches, or maybe someone else in the building also had an enemy. At this point we had other things to worry about.

It was already 7:30 and dawn was breaking. The firefighters had finally put out the fire, and the whole street smelled like burning garbage. The cops were putting NYPD sawhorses in front of the building's entrance, and they wrapped this bright yellow tape that said "CAUTION" in big black block letters, around the building's perimeter.

One of the cops posted this official NYC "No Trespassing" sign on the outside door of the building. The sign warned the derelicts and other genetic eccentrics to stay the fuck out.

All in all, the police and firemen were very kind and understanding. They told us to call the next day to find out if we could go in and salvage any of our belongings. I hoped that we could, because like most idiot tenants, I didn't have renters insurance. But, even if I did, big deal. My new problem was finding a place for me and Pamm.

I was a guy with no job and no money and an unstable girlfriend—Sure, I can find a decent one bedroom apartment in a semi-livable part of Manhattan for what I'm paying here—Sure, no problem.

Pamm and I were both frazzled to the quick. As all of the others faded from the scene, she clung to me and looked at the ground.

Then, I suddenly thought about the hundred some-odd bucks that I had in my wallet and we walked over to the Odessa. I told her to hurry up so that we wouldn't have to wait for a booth. We had nowhere else to go.

When we got to the restaurant the place was already full, with three other parties waiting for a table. Somehow the owner knew all about the fire and our misfortune, and he waved us over to the last booth in the back, the one that was always reserved for him. He hugged us both, and said that breakfast was on the house and that we could take our time.

I was touched. I mean the guy knew me, but only as a customer, and he didn't even know my name. As soon as we sat down I broke down and started to cry, that's how moved I was.

Then, Pamm started crying, but I quickly snapped out of it and looked up at her. She gave me a sheepish smile and tried to comfort me by taking my two hands in hers, and telling me all about how we could stay at this new squat just a few blocks away.

I told her to shut up and look at the menu. She kicked me under the table and I winced. Then, I smiled at her and she fished out a pack of crumpled cigarettes out of her jacket, took one out and threw the rest of the pack at me.

I picked up the matchbook that was in the ashtray and lit hers and then mine. We smoked our cigarettes and we looked around. We had a lot to talk about.

About the Author

David Steier is originally from New York City and has been a writer since his college journalism days.

Since that time, he has been published in *Mystery* magazine, and has worked as a feature editor for a New York City advertising company.

As an editor, his feature stories and publicity copy has appeared in thousands of daily newspapers across the United States.

A prodigious reader, he is especially fond of beat and neo-beat literature.

His favorite authors include William Burroughs, Hubert Selby, Jr., Charles Bukowski, and Herbert Huncke.

In fact, a chance encounter with Huncke in lower Manhattan in early 1992 helped inspire him to write this book.

His interests include photography, politics, and world travel. He currently lives in the Midwest. This is his first novel.